RENEWING LOVE

Dr. Frank and Mary Alice Minirth
Dr. Brian and Dr. Deborah Newman
Dr. Robert and Susan Hemfelt

A JANET THOMA BOOK

THOMAS NELSON PUBLISHERS
NASHVILLE

For general information about other Minirth-Meier Clinic branch offices, counseling services, educational resources, and hospital programs, call toll-free 1-800-545-1819. National Headquarters: (214)669-1733 (800)229-3000

Copyright © 1993 by Brian and Deborah Newman, Frank and Mary Alice Minirth, Robert and Susan Hemfelt

Published in Nashville, Tennessee, by Thomas Nelson, Inc., and distributed in Canada by Lawson Falle, Ltd., Cambridge, Ontario.

Scripture quotations are from the NEW KING JAMES VERSION of the Bible. Copyright © 1979, 1980, 1982, Thomas Nelson, Inc., Publishers.

Library of Congress Cataloging-in-Publication Data

Renewing Love / by Frank Minirth . . . [et al.].
        p.   cm.
        Rev. ed. of: Passages of Marriage / Frank Minirth . . . [et al.]. 1991.
        "A Janet Thoma book."
        ISBN 0-8407-4552-4
        1. Marriage—United States. 2. Communication in marriage—United States. I. Minirth, Frank B. II. Title: Passages of Marriage.
        HQ734.R355   1991
        646.7'8—dc20   *92-28814*
                                                               CIP

Printed in the United States of America
1   2   3   4   5   6   7—   99   98   97   96   95   94   93

Contents

THE AUTHORS wish to thank the many people who helped make this book possible. Many thanks to Sandy Dengler and Catharine Walkinshaw, whose writing talents brought the illustrations, thoughts, and notes from the authors to a consistent and readable form. We also thank Janet Thoma for the many hours she spent guiding, editing, and directing the completion of the manuscript. We recognize Laurie Clark and Susan Salmon for their editorial assistance and attention to the details that helped make the book complete. Lastly, we acknowledge our children: Rachel, Renee, Carrie, and Alicia Minirth; Rachel and Benjamin Newman; Katy, Kristin, and Robert Gray Hemfelt, for the special part they add to our passages through marriage.

Chapter 1

Is Your Marriage Alive and Growing?

"Over there—put the punch bowl on *that* table. Oh no! No, this will not do. Where are the flower table-cloths with pink tea roses?" In her forty-seven years, all but twenty of them married, Annie Warden Millen had learned a thing or two about making her wishes known. It's the squeaky wheel which gets the grease, the boldest lion who gets the choice. She hated coming across like a shrew, but it was the only way you got anything accomplished in life.

The wedding reception was due to start in just under three hours and every detail must be perfect. That included tablecloths.

"Oh dear! Mrs. Millen, the work order specifies white linen cloths. I'm very sorry if there was some misunderstanding," the manager of the hotel's restaurant looked ready to tug his forelock.

"When I made the arrangements, a Ms. Clark promised tablecloths with small pink tea roses on them. The color scheme, wedding and reception both, is pink and white, roses and carnations."

"And all of these sprays of roses and carnations are lovely, just lovely! Yes. I recall that the hotel has what you describe, but they're very shopworn. Very shopworn, indeed. They may have been used for last night's seafood buffet. With a buffet, you know, no one notices if the cloths look a bit tired, shall we say. Sent to linen service by now, I am very sorry . . . Ah!" the manager brightened, basking in the glow of a brilliant idea. "Pink runners! The effect will be absolutely elegant."

"Very well. I suppose that will have to do." In her forty-seven years, Annie also knew when to cut her losses and move on. She glanced at her watch and gasped. "An hour-and-a-half until the service! I've got to pick up Beth Anne. I'm holding your Ms. Clark responsible for this." She bade him good day and hurried out of the hotel, her white high heels clicking on the marble floor.

Annie had outdone herself with this wedding. Years and years of spearheading social functions—everything from church bazaars to charity benefits had prepared her for this ultimate occasion—her only daughter's wedding. All the details, the special little touches, down to the matching neckties of the limo drivers and the horse-drawn wedding carriage, were perfect. Except for the mix-up at the restaurant on the tablecloths. *Hopefully no one will notice.* Annie thought as she drove down Main street.

Beth Anne was at the hairdresser's along with all the bridesmaids. With all the giggling and whispering, the parlor sounded more like a high school restroom than a hair salon.

"Hi, Mom." Beth Anne called out. "What do you think?" Beth Anne's long blond hair tumbled in loose waves down her back with just a hint of curl. Baby's breath and pink tea roses were delicately woven through the golden strands of her hair. The effect was breathtaking.

Annie frowned. "I thought we talked about putting your hair up, in a bun, with a circlet of flowers."

"We did, but Marge recommended this. I love it, don't you?"

"It is lovely," Annie agreed, "But not very formal."

"It's perfect!" Beth Anne gushed. She jumped up from the chair and tossed her glorious mane around. "See, I can even dance and the flowers won't fall out. I can't wait until Alan sees me."

This was no time to argue with the bride. Annie bit her tongue and let this second detail slide away. And it was true; she had never seen her daughter so beautiful. Beth Anne's eyes sparkled, her cheeks flushed a delicate shade of pink. And she wasn't even wearing makeup yet.

"Well, we don't have time for any changes," Annie said. She looked in the mirror and pulled at her own neatly coiffured hair. "Let's go."

She watched the girls file out and tumble into the van. Beth Anne had chosen three close friends to be her bridesmaids. Julia Karris, a dark-haired beauty who made a striking contrast to Beth Anne's fairness. She was the matron of honor. Annie understood that Julia was on her second husband. Grace Chevington, another brunette, compared favorably with Maria Shriver in looks and intelligence. Grace was a noted newspaper reporter that Beth Anne had met through her sorority. The final bridesmaid was someone Beth Anne had just become close friends with. Still unmarried, Lisa Boraff was a pretty redhead who worked in Beth Anne's office. Her short hair fell in bouncy curls around her face. A crown of pink roses lay delicately on top. The noise level in the van on the way to the church hovered at a million decibels. Chipmunks on amphetamines.

The wedding went off without a hitch, though Annie really didn't notice. Her mind was on the reception, the last major hurdle. She just hoped the greasy restaurant manager had straightened things out. Pink runners.

The only respite from her juggling thoughts was when Beth Anne and Alan said their vows. Annie allowed herself a few tears. "How did time go so quickly?" she asked herself.

Carl and Bess Warden, Annie's parents, sat beside Annie. Bess pressed a lace handkerchief to her eyes, dabbing the tears. Carl squeezed her hand and hugged her around the shoulders. *How do they do it?* Annie thought. "Even after all these years, they act as much in love as Beth Anne and Alan."

Then she looked up at Rob, her husband. He appeared

almost handsome in his grey tuxedo. Her tears subsided. She was, so to speak, looking at him dry-eyed. Curious, how unemotional her feelings were. She was a casual bystander, he could have been one of the hotel waiters.

And her heart sighed. "Mom and Dad are happy, Beth Anne and Alan are happy. But what is happening to us?"

Time Changes

Everyone's marriage—Carl and Bess's, Annie and Rob's, Beth Anne and Alan's—changes with time. The very nature of our world causes it to be so. A couple just starting out doesn't anticipate these changes, and doesn't want to. Their eyes are blinded by the new love they have for each other.

Dr. Robert Hemfelt explains, "Most of what a couple hears in superficial pre-marital counseling goes in one ear and out the other. Many of the issues each couple will be dealing with in their lives together won't even show up until years later."

Naively, the newlyweds crow, "We'll never change!" and lace their wedding with all those songs about neverending love and devotion. Change they will. Change they must, for change is inevitable in any relationship.

You, now in your Fourth Passage, are intensely aware of those changes. And if you are like all too many couples, you lament the change time has wrought. Change, though, is not only inevitable, but desirable. "When we counsel couples," Robert Hemfelt and Brian Newman chorus together, "we consider the marriage as an individual, an entity in itself." A living, breathing thing, a marriage.

So how do you embrace the inevitable changes in marriage and make them positive? The best way is to understand what is happening and thereby redirect unpleasant changes, and reinforce the pleasant ones. We hope to show you how to redirect and reinforce with this book. A marriage that appears dull and mundane can be made to sparkle. A hopeless situation can emerge into bright promise. A good union can be made better. It all depends upon finding and managing the changes for the better. Annie Warden Millen was facing one of the biggest changes of her life, a change you face in this Fourth Passage of marriage.

Signs of Trouble

Annie surveyed the scene before her. How could such a festive event look so depressing now? Paper napkins, plastic cups, bits of food, and spilled punch littered the deserted reception hall. It was all over. Beth Anne was gone. The wedding was over. And for Annie, at this moment, her reason for living seemed over.

"Perfect to the end." Her father, Carl Warden, interrupted her sad thoughts. "Bet you're going to be glad to relax after this one."

She tried to smile; no smile came. She felt near tears again. "Dad. . ." She took a deep breath and her eyes skittered everywhere, anywhere but her father's face. "This wedding kept me busy, you might say. But now . . . now I have—I don't have anything to do. It's just Rob and me in that house all alone." She turned to her father.

"Your marriage is solid, Sugar Anne. What are you saying?" Carl studied her face with those piercing, probing eyes of his. "You always said you'd be glad to have the freedom when Beth Anne moved out."

"It's. . . ." Annie waved her hand in the air, trying to pick out words that would not come. "Rob and I—our relationship has changed somehow, Dad. He's not the same person. Or maybe I'm not. We don't have anything in common, or . . . I'm not even sure I love him anymore. And now its only me and him, me and something I don't think I want. What am I going to do, Dad?"

Hot Spots

Couples who approach professionals in our clinic rarely come in because everything is going well. Rather, they sense

trouble. They have unmet needs. Their symptoms, the surface clues to underlying problems, show up in our case files
again and again, however unique they may seem to the couples experiencing them. Because no marriage is perfect, every couple weathers these problems to some extent. But
when the problems loom too large to handle and threaten
the union, trouble will follow.

One of the biggest sources of problems that plague a couple over and over are hidden agendas. These are messages
and issues hidden deep within the subconscious mind, far
away from conscious and logical thought.

Robert Hemfelt likens hidden agendas to a time-activated
computer virus and to time-release cold capsules. Recall the
recent scare over the Michelangelo computer virus? It literally could have brought businesses and government agencies
to their knees by deleting thousands and thousands of hours
of work in one single day. Ingeniously invented, the virus
would remain dormant and undetectable until a programmed date and time activated it.

Still another example would be certain over-the-counter
cold remedies. Each capsule contains beads that dissolve at
different times over a specified period of time. The time-
release capsules Dr. Hemfelt speaks of are very similar. Life
can be chugging along comfortably for a couple when, for
no apparent reason, the relationship goes awry. The hidden
agendas, like the individual beads in the cold capsule, lay
dormant for years. Then they trigger into action by a seem-
ingly random event—Annie's daughter's wedding, for example.

During this Fourth Passage of marriage, it is true that
time-release capsules tend to be less effective because much
time has elapsed since you left your parents' home (the
source of many time-release capsules). However, a malignant hidden message may still remain, to flare up during this
passage when so many changes occur: kids leaving home and
having their own children, parents dying, and careers winding down.

Often, the root of the time-release capsule lies in unfinished business subconsciously passed on to you by your parents or even your grandparents. If you don't recognize and weed out these time-release capsules, they can be passed on to your children and your children's children. The key to stopping this legacy is to recognize and confront the agendas in your lifetime. We don't mean you must go back and solve your parents' or even your grandparents' problems. If you recognize these issues now, you can stop their problems from becoming yours. How? First you have to ferret out these issues where they hide.

In counseling and in life, we find time-release capsules kicking into action in the following areas. See if any of them sound familiar to you.

The Bedroom

Tony and Helen, married for thirty years, came into counseling to discuss their daughter Andrea. Now on her third husband, she had been caught in still another extramarital affair. What seemed on the surface like the daughter's problem actually turned out to be a hidden agenda, a time-release capsule, buried deep within the family fabric.

For our purposes here, we will only present a very brief summary of their case. We first explored Tony's, Helen's, and Andrea's past for clues. Helen's mother sent a powerful hidden message with Helen when she married Tony: "Sex is dirty within a family, sex is a wife's duty, nothing more."(This, by the way, is a very common hidden message sent with children, especially women.) Helen's mother also confided to Helen her suspicions that Helen's father had engaged in several extra-marital affairs. Within months after the wedding, sex became mechanical, unemotional, and unsatisfying for both Tony and Helen.

Tony, exasperated by Helen's coldness, found himself drawn to other women. His hidden message came from his father, who also saw other women. The message Tony received from his father was, "It's okay to seek sex outside the marital boundaries."

Since neither parent had received and developed a healthy sense of their own sexuality, Andrea was sent into the world with little or no proper information. She compulsively acted out her needs through sexual affairs. She received two hidden messages from her parents. From Mom: "Sex is illicit within a family—a marriage." Andrea's mother didn't give her an overt message to have affairs, but her mother certainly gave her negative messages about the prospects for physical intimacy within marriage. Dad's role model and message were more direct: "It's necessary to seek sex outside of marriage."

A serious problem for Andrea had its roots deeply imbedded in past generations—Andrea's parents and grandparents and their sexual mores. If we hadn't uncovered the hidden agendas, we would have just bandaged the surface cuts, while the internal infection ran its destructive course.

How did we root out the hidden agendas? First, in conversation with Helen and Tony we explored the past of each parent and grandparent, piecing together from the evidence of known events what the grandparents' and parents' true sexual attitudes must have been. Once those were out in the open, further exploration revealed the real messages hidden beneath the surface in Tony's and Helen's lives.

Only then was the daughter able to work on altering her self-destructive behavior, through inner self-talk, and by understanding the forces at war inside of her. We were able to do this because all family members had come in for counseling. This family's willingness to seek help is not the norm, however.

Obviously, it's preferable for all family members to make healthy change, but it's not always possible. In fact, it's highly improbable. The good news is, if one family member works on one issue for healthy change, a ripple effect can occur within all family members—welcomed or not. All members of a family do not have to live in the same physical area for success. A grandmother on the east coast can finally come to terms with her sexuality and grieve her losses, and then a mother on the west coast and a daughter in the south will all benefit.

Another area where we find time-release capsules or hidden agendas popping up is in financial matters.

The Checkbook

Why can't Harry get ahead? He doesn't overspend. His wife, while not frugal, is not extravagant, either. Yet his ship of finance wallows up to its gunwales in debt. By this stage in life, Harry ought to be a unit manager, if not a store manager. But he's still clerking and stocking shelves. Harry knows why he can't get ahead. He's had to change jobs five times in the last ten years because of what he perceived to be unfeeling, incompetent bosses. One of the places he worked even sent him to the company shrink to talk to him about his attitude problem. *His* attitude!

Then his wife cajoled him into marriage counseling for unrelated reasons. After a year of counseling at the Minirth-Meier Clinic in Dallas, Texas, Harry discovered a connection between his authority problems in the marriage, his authority problems with money management, and his authority conflicts with job supervisors. Harry is still in debt, but at least now the bill collectors don't call him at home and work every day. He's working things out. He says, "I went to a financial counselor long ago. But what I learned from him simply didn't work until my marriage smoothed out." He grimaces, "And I didn't even know it was wrinkled."

Not all financial distress points to marriage problems, of course. We do, however, consider chronic financial difficulties a factor that may indicate a problem. We also look closely if a person experiences constant or recurring vocational failure. This often points to some individual psychological problem or anger in the marriage.

The following is a classic example of how unresolved anger and need result in financial sabotage. A husband wanted to be married. His desire to be married was linked to the fact that a part of him longed for someone to take care of him. He buried that desire, but, he sabotaged job after job. When his work failed, he went home to his wife, to be taken care of, patched up, and shoved back into the ring. This frequent change of job was a warning signal that something was wrong. The husband's behavior was saying, "Yes, on the surface I want to be a breadwinner, but part of me yearns for someone to take care of me. I liked being a child more than I like being a responsible adult." In his case, the man never felt he was well taken care of at home, a child who never received much attention. This hidden agenda developed within his subconscious and spilled over into his marriage. Now that he and his wife see the deep messages from his past, they at last can work through and around them.

The In-Laws

A related financial clue we address is excessive monetary dependence of the married couple upon the in-laws.

"But they prepared for us with trusts and legacies!" the couple might protest.

"Fine, we're all in favor of it when inheritances are frosting on the cake." What we look for, rather, is the prospect that the couple requires that legacy in order to survive financially.

In fact, in-law problems in general suggest that unfinished business—hidden agendas—lie in the background. Severe in-law friction indicates a cross-generational problem, that, if not resolved, will fester in the present generation and infect the next ones.

We Versus They

Jason and Jennifer fight every day. They wish they didn't argue so much because it upsets the kids, just as their parents' fights used to upset them. But they believe bitter fighting is the mark of any marriage, the only way to resolve differences. Because Jennifer is "right" in most disagreements, she makes sure the kids are lined up on her side of the fence. And they tend to be on her side because Jason is unnecessarily strict with them. They naturally resent Jason's severe manner, preferring Jennifer's more easygoing ways. The fighting has moved into the bedroom, and Jennifer hasn't enjoyed their sexual expression for months. Oh, sure, Jason comes over now and then, but it's not fun anymore.

In one fell swoop, Jason and Jennifer illustrate what we look for in family imbalances: chronic fighting, sexual dysfunction, factional alliances within the family ("them" against "us"), and problems with and about kids.

Emotions

Jocelyn, a former model, fought chronic depression for years. Her husband sympathized, but he couldn't really understand her attitude. After all, he wasn't depressed. Their marriage was fine, their economic situation stable, and the in-laws were a thousand miles away. Obviously, he pointed out, it was her problem. Only when he entered into counseling with her and changed some of his own basic attitudes and behaviors did her problem disappear.

During counseling, Jocelyn's husband found that he behaved toward Jocelyn according to his upbringing. Briefly, his father had always adhered to the typical macho-male image—he never showed affection or emotion towards his wife or kids. Following this ingrained pattern, Jocelyn's husband stopped being demonstrative towards Jocelyn with his love, once courtship and the newlywed years faded away. Only when he recognized this childhood conditioning for what it was and learned to display more of his feelings to Jocelyn, was Jocelyn able to emerge from her depression. She had felt unloved for so long. Incidentally, just as had her mother-in-law before her had felt unloved.

Any emotional or psychological difficulty in one marital partner will invariably influence, and be influenced by, the other partner.

Other symptoms of marital dysfunction we look for are:

anxiety, chemical dependence and addictions, and driving compulsions such as extreme perfectionism, workaholism, spendaholism, and such. Threats of suicide are always cause for concern.

What About You?

"Nothing wrong with *my* marriage!" you boast. Good for you! There is, though, delight that comes from making a good thing better. Having nothing wrong with a marriage and improving a marriage are two different things. Fortunately, you can think of no hints of trouble in your marriage. But, nonetheless, there are rough spots to polish up in every marriage.

And then, there's your mate. Would your spouse agree with your assessment of your marital hot spots? Pause a moment and go through this list of trouble spots. Check those topics that may apply to your marriage as you see it. Add more if you need to.

_____ Problems in the Sexual Arena—between you and your spouse, or between your parents, or between your children and their spouses.

_____ Chronic Financial Distress—in your immediate family or in your extended family.

_____ In-law Problems and Involvement—overinvolvement with or alienation from yours or your spouse's parents.

_____ Family Imbalance and Stress—chronic fighting, no communication, family members taking sides in disagreements.

_____ Emotional or Psychological Dysfunctions—addictions (alcoholism, prescription drugs), depression, anxiety, or compulsions.

_____ Any thoughts or comments about suicide.

_____ Grief due to the loss of aging parents to illness, or death.

_____ Growing concern about your own physical health.

_____ Trouble allowing or encouraging your maturing children to individuate from your constant care.

_____ _____

_____ _____

If you checked any of these signs of trouble, your marriage may need some help. How about your spouse? How would he or she view each trouble sign? Has your spouse ever complained or nagged about one of these topics? Has your spouse ever seemed to go overboard with symptoms of compulsivity or depression? If so, you may have a problem you didn't know about. It's worth thinking about.

One of the biggest sources of hidden agendas—unfinished business is another term we use—is failure of a marriage (yours, your parent's, or your children's) to move from passage to passage of marriage when it should.

The Passages of Marriage

Picture yourself building a model of the clipper ship, _Cutty Sark._ (Yes, otherwise rational adults do spend many hours building tiny little ships that can't sail anywhere.) You have before you the parts and instructions. You prepare the hull and build a cradle to hold it as you work. If you don't build the cradle, you'll have trouble from that point on, because you'll have to hold the model with one hand while you work on it with the other, and many jobs take two hands.

You assemble the masts according to the directions. Hey, this looks pretty good! You drill the appropriate holes in the hull block. If you haven't put the decking on by now, you have a real problem. You'll have to back up and do that. You step the masts and at last it is starting to really look like a ship. Now you start assembling the black lines, the standing rigging. But if you haven't stepped the masts properly, the standing rigging will be wrong. And if that is wrong, you'll have a terrible time installing the running rigging, because some of the blocks and cleats attach to the standing lines. And you can't letter the hull until you've painted.

The passages of marriage are just like that. Each is a step your marriage must make in sequence. One step must be completed before the next step commences, or the new step will be negatively influenced in some way.

When a marriage—that living, breathing entity—gets stalled in a passage, it ceases growing, and dies.

By definition, then, *passages are predictable and necessary stages, involving the physical, the emotional, and the spiritual.* Through them, partners journey toward the lifetime goal of growth as individuals and as a couple.

In our personal lives and in our professional practice, the six authors of this book have identified five distinct stages, passages through which marriage progresses. The developmental stages through which a child passes from birth into adulthood are well known. Similarly, a marriage matures from developmental stage to stage—from passage to passage —according to the number of years it has existed. Remarriage may differ somewhat; because the partners have been married previously, they might telescope a passage into a briefer time, or extend a passage beyond its normal life span. In general, though, marriages hew closely to the following outline:

- The First Passage—New Love: the first two years / Whether the couple are eighteen years old or eighty, they pass first through this dewy-eyed stage of idealized love. Persons who have been married previously may go through this stage a little faster than those married for the first time, but everyone tastes its heady joy.
- The Second Passage—Realistic Love: from the second anniversary through the tenth / Kids and career put the push on. About now, too, a heavy dose of reality sets in. This perfect partner is not so perfect after all. If this is Eden, why the thorns?
- The Third Passage—Steadfast Love: from the tenth anni-

versary through the twenty-fifth / Wrapped up in career, kids, and a host of extraneous, time-consuming activities, the couple find themselves in a rut. Either they're mushing along complacently or at each other's throats, but there's a predictability about the whole thing.

Change is necessary and change is desirable.

- The Fourth Passage—Renewing Love: from the twenty-fifth through the thirty-fifth anniversary / As the kids fledge and the career peaks out, the meaning and purpose of life alters forever. Now what?
- The Fifth Passage—Transcendent Love: beyond the thirty-fifth anniversary / What a history this couple has! The texture of the marriage changes as the couple enter retirement and watch youth fade forever.

As your marriage moves from one of these passages to another, growing and developing along the way, like your ship model, it also moves through specific conditions common to the human condition. Crisis and conflict, intimacy, forgiveness, children, and memories form some of them.

The tasks which define each passage must be completed before the next passage's tasks commence. By tasks we mean attitude changes one must make and jobs one must complete in order to maintain an intimate marital relationship. Page (28) shows the passages and tasks that must be completed for a marriage to complete its lifetime journey toward intimacy.

Should your ship model be stranded in some major way, you must either rip way back and essentially start over, or throw it out. If you choose to go back and correct the errors, you may need the counsel of someone who understands more about ship modeling than you do. When it comes to marriage, we never recommend throwing it out. Throwing it out is not only wasteful but extremely painful, particularly in the Fourth Passage; you've put so much time and effort into your marriage, invested so much of yourself. Carl and Bess Warden, married forty-eight years, were completing a very satisfying model. As painful as eventual separation and death would be, the Wardens both would know the peace and satisfaction of being able to say, "We did it."

One of every two married couples will never know that satisfaction.

During their long life together, Carl and Bess Warden did not talk to marriage counselors or become involved in marriage therapy of any sort, though counseling might have helped them navigate the difficult passages more easily. Yet Carl and Bess did not simply muddle through. They worked diligently at their marriage. To the very end, Carl and Bess enjoyed the fruits of a growing, timeless, abiding love.

Annie and Rob Millen, married twenty-eight years, were seeing their ship model all askew. They were stuck in a tough construction phase and neither could see a way out. Their marriage had lost its vigor and, for Annie, its purpose. What went wrong? We hear their story too often in counseling. Their challenge would be to make it through the Fourth Passage. After all, they had made it this far, the end was in sight, worth shooting for, even with gusto!

You may be thinking, *But my marriage is so different; nobody has a husband like mine, or a wife like mine.*

Don't be so sure.

What If My Marriage Doesn't Fit the Pattern?

Some cheese factories provide tours. In Tillamook, Oregon, for example, you can wander along an elevated catwalk, watching the cheese-making below. You see the workers pour milk into huge rectangular tanks. You watch them stir the mixture, then cut huge slabs of curds. They age the cheese according to what the desired end product will be. Some cheeses must cure for months. Others are ready quickly and will spoil within days. Aging is the key to cheese-making, it cannot be hastened. The effects of time are uniform on cheese. They are also uniform on marriages. The patterns of time prevail even though yours may be a most unusual union. In fact, what is "normal"?

Mary Alice and Frank Minirth know their marriage could probably never be considered normal. "When we married, we were both in school," Mary Alice explains. "Frank, in medical school, studied day and night. I had two years yet to complete my degree, so I was studying too. It wasn't a normal start-a-family situation.

"My first job was as a teacher in inner-city Little Rock. Definitely not normal! Frank worked a twenty-five-hour day completing his internship. Then, getting a practice started—not normal. Possibly, there's no such thing as a normal marriage."

Your own situation may be less stressful than the Minirths', or more stressful. You may be fishing off the Alaskan coast or working in a bank in Topeka. What's normal?

The passages themselves are the norm, the common denominators of any marriage. They form the skeleton upon which problems and pleasures attach.

Each of the authors of this book is at a different passage: Brian and Debi Newman in the Second Passage, Robert and Susan Hemfelt just approaching the Third Passage, and Frank and Mary Alice Minirth in the Fourth. We will share with you our personal experiences as well as our professional insights. In addition to counseling couples and leading marriage enrichment seminars, psychotherapists Brian and Debi put their advanced degrees to work on the staff of the Minirth-Meier Clinic. Dr. Minirth, psychiatrist and a cofounder of the clinic, takes special interest in marriage and family dynamics. Dr. Robert Hemfelt, psychologist, is well known and respected as a leader in the study of codependency and multigenerational issues.

Before we begin this book in depth, a brief review of the passages passed through up to this point is warranted. Take a moment to reminisce, back to the early days of your marriage, back to your wedding day . . .

The First Passage

In a breathless moment, the wedding day comes and goes. A lifetime of promise stretches out before the happy couple. They tiptoe around each other tenuously working out such issues as decision making, conflict, intimacy and independence. If they successfully pass through this First Passage, they have established an identity and home away from their parents.

Look at page 28. If you see any tasks under this First Passage that you may not have accomplished, we invite you to read, *New Love* (Nashville: Thomas Nelson, 1993), the first in this series on the passages of marriage. Rounding first base, the couple runs into second base and comes face to face with the second baseman—reality.

Since many readers may read only one book in this series, we have repeated certain key concepts in more than one book. If you encounter this repetition, please be open to the possibility that these subjects are so vital, they bear such repetition.

The Second Passage

"The honeymoon is over" is a good phrase for what happens to a marriage in this reality phase. The marriage is in full swing now. Kids and careers make major time and energy demands. Too, the marriage partners now get a good, hard look at what kind of person they really married. That reality is too much for most couples as the highest divorce rate hovers during this period. The seven-year itch—it's no myth.

With all this bad news, it would seem that no marriage can make it through this difficult period. Thankfully, many do. What sets those apart are the tasks that are successfully accomplished to pass beyond this base: Staying in love even when reality strikes, childproofing the marriage so that the marriage remains the building block for the family, and weeding out and facing the hidden agendas, time-release capsules that are at work trying to bring the marriage down.

Those hidden agendas we discussed earlier start popping into action in this Second Passage. If recognized and dealt with here, they will become less damaging in future passages. If not, they will recur over and over and will loom even larger on your marriage. Peruse the tasks under the Second Passage on page 28 and see how well you've accomplished them. If you have any questions about these tasks, we invite you to read, *Realistic Love* (Nashville: Thomas Nelson, 1993), the second book in this series. A victorious marriage makes it through this battletorn passage and looks forward to the third.

The Third Passage

After ten or so many years of being together the couple knows each other very well, sometimes too well. This passage is marked by complacency, comfort, and familiarity. Each partner knows the other so well, he or she can almost read the other's thoughts. The challenge of this passage is to walk the tightrope between malignant dependency and estranged independence. Both of these lead to codependency —a real threat in the Third Passage.

At this stage of life the couple is also dealing with teenagers, truly the biggest parental challenge. If the marriage has not successfully mastered the tasks of the First and Second Passages, the teen years will be difficult.

While the couple may be wrestling with their own children, they may also be wrestling with their parents. That relationship is changing, hopefully for the better. For now, your parents, if still alive, are your peers. No longer are they demi-gods, there to bail you out of any mess. In fact, you may now be bailing them out of a few messes.

Add to these changes, the inevitable changes of your body and your spouse's. The aging process is more apparent now. Unrealized dreams—financial, career, and personal—are glaringly obvious.

The Third Passage can be immensely uplifting if the tasks are successfully accomplished. A couple can emerge from this passage into the Fourth with a promise for enhanced intimacy, togetherness, and happiness.

Look at page 28. Have you and your spouse successfully completed the tasks under the Third Passage? Are there any doubts, questions? If so, read *Steadfast Love* (Nashville: Thomas Nelson, 1993), for the answers.

Now that we've said that time is the key, we note that there are a few circumstances in which not everyone will follow exactly to this time frame. Some persons, marrying late, telescope passages, though not necessarily by choice. Changes in life seem to happen to them quicker. Other couples, delaying children, convolute passages.

These days people are getting married and then having babies decades apart from their peers. Women are delaying children until their careers have reached a point where they can afford to take the time to have a baby. It's not unusual for a couple to be married more than twenty years and be raising small children.

That's not negative, but it changes the marriage passages picture a bit. Couples who are getting a late start on some things like children will be hit by factors of different passages all at once. On the plus side, a couple who is older in age or whose marriage is further along is more mature and able to handle the stress better.

Susan Hemfelt explains, "Older couples are more likely to move through the passages more quickly for several reasons. They want to be at the same place as people who married younger, and they're more mature to start with. They have a strong personal identity. They've been out on their own for awhile."

Thus, the tasks of the passages don't have to be accomplished one at a time. Work can be done on several tasks at once. However, no matter how it's done, every marriage must master the tasks of each passage before it can successfully move forward.

This Book—The Fourth Passage

Annie Warden Millen sat in her living room working on a needlepoint first-anniversary sampler for Beth Anne. She looked across at Rob, who was watching the game on television. "What's on?" she asked.

"Huh?" her husband grunted.

"What are you watching?"

"The NBA play-offs."

"Who's playing?"

"The Trailblazers and the Bulls."

"Where are they from?"

"Portland and Chicago. Now for Pete's sake, Annie, I'm trying to watch the game . . . Oh no . . . he fouled out. Just great! Now they have to sub!" Rob pounded the armrest and turned up the sound.

Annie sighed. Rob's interest in needlepoint was about as great as her interest in Bullblazers, or whatever they were. *What in heaven's name are we ever going to talk about now that Beth Anne is gone? Do we have any common ground?* she wondered.

That thought terrified Annie as it does many couples entering their Fourth Passage of marriage. We hope to show you, in the following pages, ways to tap the riches of this passage and unearth a love even stronger than the day you were married.

Everyone knows that men come back from wars intimately tied to their comrades—for conflict and tribulation build bonds, strong bonds. That's exactly why reunions of this battalion and that unit are so popular. After twenty-five years of a life together, your bond is equally as ripe for strengthening. Surviving and conquering challenges is an avenue to this strength. It begins with deflecting the arrows that life throws at us.

Major Tasks of All the Passages of Marriage

THE FIRST PASSAGE–NEW LOVE
(The First Two Years of Marriage)

Task 1: Mold into One Family
Task 2: Overcome the Tendency to Jockey for Control
Task 3: Build a Sexual Union
Task 4: Make Responsible Choices
Task 5: Deal with Your Parents' Incomplete Passages

THE SECOND PASSAGE–REALISTIC LOVE
(From the Second Anniversary through the Tenth)

Task 1: Hang on to Love After Reality Strikes
Task 2: Childproof Your Marriage
Task 3: Recognize the Hidden Contracts in Your Marriage
Task 4: Write a New Marriage Contract

THE THIRD PASSAGE–STEADFAST LOVE
(From the Tenth Anniversary through the Twenty-fifth)

Task 1: Maintain an Individual Identity along with the Marriage Identity
Task 2: Say the Final Good-byes
Task 3: Overcome the Now-or-Never Syndrome
Task 4: Practice True Forgiveness
Task 5: Accept the Inevitable Losses
Task 6: Help Your Adolescent Become an Individual
Task 7: Maintain an Intimate Relationship

THE FOURTH PASSAGE–RENEWING LOVE
(From the Twenty-fifth Anniversary through the Thirty-fifth)

Task 1: Combat the Crisis of This Passage
Task 2: Reestablish Intimacy
Task 3: Grieve the Particular Losses of This Passage

THE FIFTH PASSAGE–TRANSCENDENT LOVE
(Beyond the Thirty-fifth Anniversary)

Task 1: Prepare for Retirement
Task 2: Continue Renewing Love
Task 3: Achieve a Transcendent Perspective
Task 4: Accept My One and Only God-given Life

Chapter 2

Can You Overcome the Slings and Arrows of Life?

A nnie Millen was headed for a serious illness. She wasn't diagnosed as having some disease. Nor had she been breathed upon by a busload of germ-laden schoolchildren. No external indications suggested she was likely to become ill. But she had placed herself under extreme stress these last few months, handling the wedding and her job, and burying her doubts about her marriage. Suddenly that stress was lifted, and Beth Anne was married. Stress reduction was a very positive change for Annie, but it was a change all the same. The empty nest was a neutral change for her—Beth Anne had been living on her own for two years, so "empty nest" was not the best term—but her status was a change. She was now a mother-in-law. Annie was coming to grips with the emptiness of her relationship, and that was, on the surface, a change for the worse.

Change, whether positive, negative, or neutral, can actually trigger illness, if too much comes at once. It is *not* "all in your head." You body chemistry actually shifts, causing physical symptoms of illness and lowering your resistance to disease.

So powerful is stress, some researchers have set up a numerical system, assigning stress points for various crises. In one of the most popular of these systems, the top three stressors—divorce and separation, the death of a spouse, the

death of a child—are all relational. The bereaved feel a loss
of intimacy, a sense of isolation. Marriage provides the best
insulation against crisis (married men live significantly longer
than do unmarried men), and marriage creates the most
profound stress when it goes wrong.

According to the rating system, retiring, losing your job,
starting a new job, getting sick, even moving to a new
home, all cause stress. Any drastic shift in the status quo
upsets more than just your routine. Good changes work as
much havoc as bad ones. Winning the lottery is about as bad
for you as going bankrupt. Getting married scores many
stress points. So does parenthood, or marrying off a child.

Taken one or two at a time, all these kinks in the plow-line
of life cause little more than temporary problems. When several of them hit you at once, the points add up and trouble
follows. Their power can overwhelm you.

The Fourth Passage of marriage is such a prime time for
major life transitions—career plateau, children leaving
home, health changes—that the cumulative stress may be
higher than you might first assume.

Not all stressors and crises are recognized as such, at least
not at the time they happen. As Mary Alice Minirth points
out, "Uncles who came back from World War II shaped the
generations that followed. Many of them had the anger and
frustration we called Post-Traumatic Stress, though it wasn't
recognized then, it shaped how their families were raised.
They weren't fathers in our modern sense. Everyone now is
into 'Let's be good fathers.' But to that generation, back
from war, father went out and supported the family and that
was all. The roles were rigid, and they were stressful.

"The Depression and World War II together fostered a lot
of uncontrollable stress, so that everyone felt like a survivor:
'We did our thing and we made it.' That could be a whole
book, just on how the thirties and forties shaped us. Because
then came the 'Me' generation."

Things that seem simple—"piece of cake!"—produce
stress. One of those stressors is nothing less than your move-

ment from passage to passage through your marriage. You can't avoid it. The crises come when the rules of the game shift but the referee doesn't tell you. Spouses' attitudes and priorities must change to fit the changing nature of the marriage, but there's no clear indicator as to how or when. Sometimes the two partners fail to change at the same time. One, still wrapped securely in the First Passage, may be drooling at the thought of romance while the other, having moved on to the passage of reality, is getting a little bored with this whole scene. In short, the abrupt changes that always happen in real life can easily unhorse marriage partners, whether or not the partners know the changes are happening.

To an extent, stressors are what you make them. "Oh no!" shrieks the young teen. "I'm doomed!" Her crisis? A pimple just prior to a major date. To her, it's serious. To Dad, it's all a joke . . . until the picture tube blows just as he plans to watch a major sporting event. ("So what?" muses the daughter.) Overreaction and underreaction, like beauty, are in the eye of the beholder. But the crisis exists in any case.

Acne outbreak or plague outbreak, crisis must be met one way or another. Actually, there is more than one way to meet crisis. Susan Hemfelt points out, "There are three ways to address a problem: the all, the nothing, and the large gray area. Ideally, you tackle every problem with a comprehensive 'all' solution. That's the best solution possible to the problem. The 'nothing' approach is ignoring the problem, or getting stubborn, or going into denial, or maybe taking the wrong track.

"Then there's the broad gray area that's a bandage for the situation. It's not going to cure anything. You're not actually solving the problem, you're just putting it off temporarily. The problem will show up again, maybe worse next time. But you have to do something immediately, so you put on a bandage. It's not the 'all' solution, but it's not the 'nothing' one, either."

Crises arise in every passage of marriage, of course, but they seem to have more profound implications as you grow older. A crisis you could bounce back from in youth becomes overwhelming at a later age. You have little time left of your life to repair some crises—financial setback, personal problems, or career difficulties. Therefore, crisis becomes a major task. Handling it well is an important goal.

The First Task: To Combat the Crises of This Passage

Imagine a squirrel clambering about in a tree. Claws scratching in the bark, the squirrel scampers up the main trunk. Soon the squirrel has two options: climb out this first major limb, or continue up toward the other limbs. Should the squirrel move out onto that bottom limb, a large part of the tree is out of reach, for it can't get to the rest of tree from here. The squirrel makes a choice between this branch and the next. That's what life is all about, making decisions —choosing a branch. The challenge is to choose the right branch so you don't get hung out on a limb.

Now what if a pine marten comes scrabbling up the trunk in hot pursuit—crisis! Will the squirrel end up as the marten's lunch? The squirrel dashes up the nearest branch, out the closest twig. It hangs, bobbing, on the very end of the branch. With a valiant lunge it leaps five feet to another branch and skitters onto a whole different limb system to make its escape.

The squirrel, pressed by circumstance, had little choice. It got away the best it could, not via the preferred escape route but out the quickest, nearest, escape route.

Similarly, persons faced by crisis may have precious little choice in how to respond. The choice is made for them by circumstance and their own nature. The squirrel, for example, could not fly away as would a blue jay. Different people respond, naturally, in different ways (based as much on their hidden agendas as on their natures, incidentally), and the reaction is automatic. It's the first and quickest thing to do, not necessarily the best.

Some persons slip instantly into denial. This isn't always bad. At times, couples need a measure of temporary denial. For example, let's examine such a situation with clients of ours, James and Lonna Jorgensen. They lost their third child, two-year-old Joci, in a tragic battle with cancer. One of the most severe losses a couple can suffer, the death of a child, crushed James so thoroughly and instantly, he couldn't even call the relatives to tell them. Lonna did the phoning. She made the funeral arrangements. She maintained a stiff upper lip. As James came to terms with their loss, she kept the family going. Six months later she fell apart and James couldn't figure out why. After all, it happened and it was over with. James had worked it through; he was well along with his grieving. He didn't understand that Lonna, having hidden the truth behind a thick layer of denial, was just now beginning to grieve. Denial is a necessary part of the grieving process. Only when it is carried to extreme does it become malignant.

Some persons respond by giving up. "Giving up" means anything from walking away from the problem and going fishing to committing suicide.

Some people respond to crises by more than just unresolved anger. They become trapped in an addiction, either by itself or in conjunction with other responses. People with a history of codependency problems are especially vulnerable to addictions, obsessions, and compulsions.

Some turn against God. "If He really loved me . . . It's His fault. He's omnipotent; He could have prevented this."

Some turn against their mates. We see many cases of a person in crisis blaming the spouse, fairly or unfairly.

And some people, to the enormous benefit of their marriages, turn not against their spouses, but toward them. That is the positive way, the method of surmounting crisis that leads to a stronger marriage and healthier relationship.

The Minirths dealt with major losses in the past—deaths

of loved ones, miscarriages—and they deal with loss and crisis today. So do the Newmans. So do the Hemfelts, who have lost parents and others. So do you.

Not every crisis resolves itself satisfactorily. Not every squirrel finds an escape route. Let us assume for the balance of this chapter that your marriage has already been damaged by crisis. If it has not (and few have not), you will still find this recovery model useful for ironing out the little wrinkles as well.

For purposes of the exercise, think of a crisis or problem that caused friction recently in your own marriage. It might be that your company has forced you into early retirement, or demoted you, or downscaled your job. For convenience, let's name that incident "IT." Work through IT along with us as we describe the process we use at the clinic to help patients deal with crises.

This process consists of ten steps, some very brief and others lengthy and difficult. From time to time, you may find yourself recycling through one or more of them as additional issues emerge.

Step 1: Suspend the Blame Cycle

Dr. Frank Minirth sits back in his chair and shakes his head sadly. "I'm dealing with a case where the husband, John, wants a divorce. He has a wonderful family with three kids, a good wife. He's leaving all that because he found someone else. He's back in that First Passage again, searching for romantic, idealistic love.

"In my office this man goes on and on about what's wrong with his wife, Gloria. He's projecting his own frustrations and shortcomings on her, you see. I can't imagine him in the future getting very far with his new love either. He's not taking any responsibility for his own problems."

Luckily, this story has a happy ending. Let's see how the satisfactory resolution came about.

John laid all his woes at Gloria's door. It was her fault he was seeking love elsewhere, he said. She was no longer as responsive, no longer as sympathetic. A man needs what a man needs and she just wasn't delivering.

In large part, that is what blame is. The blamer projects his or her own pains and frustrations onto the projection screen of the spouse. It's easy to do. By focusing all that blame on someone else, the blamer escapes the white heat of the spotlight on his or her own actions.

As John did, you must first suspend that blame cycle. No longer do you seek in someone else's actions the source of your own misery. Tackling this man's problems in a clinic setting, we asked both John and Gloria to take this first step. Which of them actually should be taking the blame? The wife, of course, would say, "It's his fault! He's the one who wants out." Neither, from this point on, is assigned blame. Rather, both are urged to assume healthy responsibility for their contributions to the pain.

We counsel numbers of couples who are working through Fourth Passage crises. A couple with a problem you may be experiencing now we'll call Larry and Beverly. Larry had been a research manager. He handled product research and development, and directed the company's retooling. One day his company told him, essentially, "For the last ten years until your retirement, you will train field sales representatives to sell our newest equipment." It was their polite way of saying, "We're really through using you for major work. We're going to keep you on the payroll, but we're doing it out of legal obligation, not because we need you. We don't want you suing us for age discrimination, but Larry, boy, you've lost the cutting edge."

His wife Beverly had originally gone into real estate as a lark, something else to do after all those years of staying home with the kids. She earned her license and started out in suburban first-home deals. Within a few years she was handling industrial real estate involving some major bucks. Now her mounting success had become an issue between them.

Blame often surfaces in indirect ways. Larry didn't outwardly blame his wife for his demotion. Were you to ask him, he'd say it was ridiculous. And to the logical mind, it is. Inside, however, he laid the fault at her door, at his company's door, perhaps even at God's. He was still good, still sharp. They were missing a good deal, dumping him off the R & D team.

His hurt turned inward into depression, and that surfaced as anger and a critical attitude. He projected much of it onto his wife: she was handy, you see, and an intimate part of him. Because of the unique intimacy of the married couple, self-blame and spouse-blame are nearly the same.

Nothing his wife did was right. He criticized her housekeeping, her cooking, and the hours she devoted to her career, even though he had originally encouraged her to try real estate. Finally, he began to sabotage her work indirectly.

When Beverly wanted to rent some office space outside the home, Larry warned her about the high overhead, about the volatility of real estate. "Let's salt away the money you would be spending on office rent." Underneath he was saying, "You're riding a wave, you know. A fad. You're just a woman; do you really know how tough it is out there in the business world? Your current success is probably just a fluke." None of that was voiced openly. Larry didn't fully realize he thought those things. But the message came across to Beverly below conscious level. Talk about bursting someone's balloon!

In the crisis or problem you put in mind at the beginning of this section, IT, how could you be expressing the blame you feel or how is your spouse expressing it? (Larry, who was demoted, for instance, also became more controlling about general household issues, such as finances. Suddenly, he began scrutinizing all his wife's expenses, even though together they were now making more money than ever before.)_____

_____

At whose door was the blame laid?_____

Does this person deserve the full weight of the blame?__

What personal responsibility do I need to accept?_____

John was doing the same with Gloria. The question is not, does she/he deserve it? The question is, is it happening?

Step 2: Acknowledge Your Contribution to the Pain

John had to examine his own actions. How was he hurting his wife? His kids? Business associates? Parents? People who looked to him as a leader? He was certainly not acting in a vacuum. What were his own shortcomings? "None," he said at first. And we invited him, ever so politely, to look again.

Larry and Beverly's kids were grown and out of the house, but Larry was still doing immense damage. He was hurting Beverly and the relationship. Beverly, in turn, was distancing herself from Larry, building a life without him in it. There is a balance here between separation of self and unity with another, and Beverly was off the balance on the separation end.

As you think about that recent incident in your life, you will see that IT affects both partners and probably other people as well.

List two persons hurt by IT and how they were hurt (For instance, Larry greatly hurt his wife with his constant criticism and undermining):
1._____
He or she was hurt in this way:_____
2._____
He or she was hurt in this way:_____

What peripheral damage was done by IT—loss of money, time, effort, prestige?_____
_____
_____

Now the big-ticket question: How much of that pain and

loss could have been avoided or minimized had you acted differently?

_____

_____

That's your contribution to the crisis.

Once Larry had acknowledged his contribution to the pain in his marriage, he also had to admit his own fear and vulnerability. Finally, in one session he was able to turn to Beverly and say, "I am afraid. I feel inadequate. I am scared about my long-term ability to provide for our family."

"I" statements, such as these, are not blame statements, which always begin with the word *you*. Instead of the previous blame statements ("Your job is insecure. You are taking too much control of our marriage."), Larry was now, as we say in the trade, owning his pain. "Yes, I have begun to be hypercritical and overcontrolling as a way to mask my fear and insecurity." Once he admitted this, his inappropriate actions were no longer necessary.

Step 3: Examine the Status of Your Marriage: Have You Negotiated All the Tasks in Each Passage So Far?

John was not ready to admit that he was hung up in the First Passage, seeking that new love. He certainly denied Dr. Minirth's counsel that if he couldn't make it into later passages with this wife, he'd likely not with the new lady either.

Gloria was just as recalcitrant. "I'm not the problem," she insisted. "John is." She had to go back and do step one all over again; she had to suspend blame. How are you doing with step one? Got it in hand? Good.

In the case of Larry, the demoted R & D man, we helped him and Beverly both to see that they had never gone beyond the earliest, most rudimentary contract for a marriage. Larry's version of their contract said, in effect, "The man has purpose in this marriage only as long as he is a strong breadwinner."

How did you do on our quiz of the passages in Chapter 1?

Have you both accomplished and mastered the tasks of Passages One, Two, and Three? If there are areas of doubt, we invite you to read any of the first three books in this series: *New Love* (Nashville: Thomas Nelson, 1993), the First Passage of Marriage; *Realistic Love* (Nashville: Thomas Nelson, 1993), the Second Passage; and, *Steadfast Love* (Nashville: Thomas Nelson, 1993), the Third Passage.

Through this process, Larry found out that he never worked through the Second Passage task of understanding his individual identity within the marriage relationship. He needed to look for other identities in his marriage relationship besides being a successful breadwinner. He might identify spiritual leadership, companionship, tenderness. A major part of his healing would be to discover these other roles and functions in his marriage.

Step 4: Commit to Recovery and Determine to Improve Your Marriage

That sounds easy. "We wouldn't be doing this if we weren't committed to recovery," you protest. But we didn't say, "Explore the option of recovery." Commitment means you're going to do it, no matter what comes. Exactly how much time are you willing to devote (a generalized "whatever it takes" won't cut it here; be specific)? Exactly what sort of program are you willing to enter? What options will you *not* commit to? Now is the time to put your recovery into clear perspective.

Larry made a verbal commitment to go back and look at his family-of-origin so he could understand why he had such a one-dimensional view of masculinity. Then he would look for new and different ways to be a part of this marriage team.

We suggest that you declare such a commitment yourself by signing one of these two statements:

"I am willing to commit fully to working through our problems. I don't mean to simply muddle through, but to work diligently toward resolution and an improved life together."

(signed) _____

"I will not commit fully to working through our problems. Muddling through is enough. If resolution never comes, it never comes. That's life."

(signed) _____

Step 5: Assess How Much Deep Sharing Goes on Between You

Yours, mine, ours. Which is which? When approached with this question, John said, "My marriage is a sharing arrangement. That's not the problem." Everybody says that.

We're not talking about who scrubs the toilet and who mows the lawn. We're talking about letting the spouse know of your needs and expecting to see them met. We're talking about listening to your spouse and trying to meet the needs you hear about.

Frequently, we find people whose needs have gone unmet so long and so often, they have given up asking, or even wanting, anymore.

- "What's the use? I never get it anyway."
- "I shouldn't have to ask for it. My spouse should know I need this." (That was Beverly's complaint. John had voiced support of her return to a career. Now he should know exactly what he must do in the way of support, without being told every step of the way.)

Both attitudes are barriers to intimacy. Both spawn crisis where no crisis would otherwise be. With them, anger smolders into resentment and bitterness. This is why we emphasize ways to prevent anger from becoming resentment and bitterness by employing forgiveness as an essential daily tool.

The communication between Larry and Beverly had become minimal as her job picked up momentum and as the anger and pain from his demotion increased. No changes had been made in their day-to-day lifestyle even though her responsibilities had increased and his job had scaled down. Together they needed to adjust the household duties to meet these changes.

What are your needs?

_____ More sexual release?

_____ Less?

_____ More affection?

_____ More attention?

_____ More trust in matters of finance?

Now, what about your spouse? What unmet needs have you and your spouse contributed, or are contributing, to IT?

_____

_____

_____

Decide which needs are most important and then talk to your spouse about them.

Step 6: Employ Loving Confrontation After You Have Securely and Completely Suspended the Blame Cycle

Boy, do we hear the jibes and word plays on "loving confrontation!" It is not a boxing match with heart-shaped gloves, or a brawl with a smile pasted on. Only after _both_ parties have willingly suspended blame, and kept it suspended, can we hope for success here.

One at a time, each expresses concerns and reservations to the other. Each tells the other how that person is or is not meeting needs.

Larry's wife did exactly that. In a counseling session, Beverly told him he wasn't hearing what the company was telling him. Even though he had been demoted, and even been told his new job would be less demanding, he had worked longer hours in the last few months than ever before. We saw this as a form of magical thinking: _If I just work hard enough or improve my working ability enough, I won't be phased out._

"These added work hours are ripping our marriage even

Crisis Management

STEP 1: Suspend the blame cycle.

STEP 2: Acknowledge your contribution to the pain.

STEP 3: Examine the status of your marriage: Have you negotiated all the tasks in each passage to date?

STEP 4: Commit to recovery and determine to improve your marriage.

STEP 5: Assess how much deep sharing goes on between you: Are needs being met?

STEP 6: Employ loving confrontation, after you have securely and completely suspended the blame cycle.

STEP 7: Grieve the pain in your marriage.

STEP 8: Meet needs through a series of "give-and-take" sessions

STEP 9: Commit to repairing the future as well as the present.

STEP 10: Minimize the stressors in your marriage. Like a tidal wave, they come a bit at a time, one here and one there. It's their cumulative toll that gets you. The most powerful tidal wave is composed of droplets.

further apart," Beverly said. "I'd like to see you home more, now that you have more time."

In your confrontation, each of you should tell the other what you would like to see.

What action (or actions) do you want your mate to take now?

_____

_____

_____

What actions would have helped alleviate the crisis situation?

_____

Consider also the general marriage state.

What do you feel is missing from this marriage union? Is there anything you feel you have a little too much of?

This is the time to bring up fears about specific issues such as possible chemical dependency or growing estrangement. Gently and with care, you air trouble spots and potential trouble spots you see in the marriage.

What rocks lie in the road to bliss? _____

Step 7: Grieve the Pain in Your Marriage

Effective grieving requires five separate steps, and you have to go through each one of them to completely resolve a loss. Grieving is so fundamental to life and to a healthy marriage that we will refer to it frequently. You may recycle back through each step several times or you may get stuck in one step for a period of time. But you must progress through all the steps before you can say you've completely grieved the loss. And you can't shortcut the process, skip over a step, or talk your way through one. We find persons in our counsel looking over the grieving steps and saying, "Okay, I've worked through all those steps. I felt sadness, I cried. I got mad." But they actually were still in the process of grieving, stalled in the step of bargaining. Saying they had grieved the loss and assuming it was done with meant, for them, that the issue was resolved.

Think of grieving as a process, a dynamic one. Grief is commonly associated with sadness, but sadness is only one step in the process. In actuality, it's very cleansing, refreshing, the aftermath of a ferocious thunderstorm. The five steps of grieving, almost universally recognized by clinicians, are:

1. Shock and Denial—Anger is appropriate here. "How could so and so do that to me?"

2. Depression—You may feel hopeless, down all the time. Expect depression, it's a normal part of grieving. However, if depression becomes severe or lingers for weeks or months, seek medical help.

3. Bargaining—Bargaining and magical thinking are natural parts of grieving, but they should be temporary. Don't let them become plans of action: "If I change the way I'm acting toward him/her, maybe he'll/she'll not treat me so badly." Wrong. The person in this case must grieve the pain from this hurt and recognize these words as bargaining. Then go on to the next step.

Larry was exercising magical thinking, below conscious level. "If I work harder and do more, they'll change their minds and promote me." A deeper bargain Larry harbored with himself: "If I struggle back to the top of my household and my job, the hurt will leave."

John practiced his own bargaining. "If I can just start over with this new woman, I will be happy."

Until both men employed their bargaining as part of the grieving process, the bargaining availed nothing.

4. Sadness—This differs from depression. Remember the couple, James and Lonna Jorgenson, who lost their daughter to cancer? When Lonna finally went through the grieving process, her sadness hit after the depression and the shock. For a period of time, she was deeply sorrowful over her daughter's death. Her sadness angered and hurt James, who had nearly completed his own grieving process. James then faced the necessity of grieving his anger. It damaged the marriage bond. Therefore it was a loss.

5. Forgiveness, Acceptance, and Resolution—This is the light at the end of the tunnel, the rainbow after the storm. It brings a measure of peace, but it doesn't erase the memories.

Lonna found peace and healing when she finally forgave God for taking their daughter.

John and Gloria, struggling with infidelity, had to grieve the pain this caused to their marriage, utilizing this process. But there was other pain, pain from the past, that had to be handled as well.

"What pain?" John grumbled.

"I don't want to talk about it," Gloria said. In truth, there was deep personal pain in their lives, in addition to the infidelity there were other deeply buried issues from their marriage history. Gloria's first pregnancy ended in miscarriage. It was years ago. Afraid of what to say or do, John said and did nothing. Because men aren't supposed to come all apart over something like that, he refused to recognize any emotional reaction in himself, and he felt uncomfortable when she tried to talk about it.

"That's history. Years ago!" he told her in couples counseling. "You're beating a dead horse." It was history, all right. It was an unmet need in Gloria that had been festering for a long time. Because he refused to participate in the grieving, she herself did not grieve the loss adequately (though, had she realized, she could have proceeded on her own with that). Until they both went back and dealt with that buried issue, it would continue to generate resentment. It was primarily that issue which kept Gloria in a chronic depression. And it was the fruit of her depression, coldness and lackluster feelings, that John cited as his reason for straying. This unclosed bit of history caused much, much pain.

Any chronically unmet needs, as well as pain not dealt with, must be purged by bringing them into the open and grieving them through. "You're just stirring up issues that would die by themselves if left alone!" John fumed. "No," we assured him, "they will not die if left alone. They will fester. And they will spread poison. That's the whole point of this."

"These items hurt at the time, but I put them behind me."

After Beverly confronted Larry, he was able to grieve about his job change and to grieve the destruction this crisis had caused in their marriage. Once he grieved the demotion he could accept it and make peace with his new situation.

What is the pain in your marriage? Think about lost lives, lost opportunities, lost affections—even lost pets, if pets were important to you. Think about disappointments, which are losses of a different sort. And unmet dreams, all these losses must be grieved.

1. _____
2. _____
3. _____

Sooner or later you must deal with them, then put them behind you.

Step 8: Meet Needs Through a Series of "Give-and-Take" Sessions

What am I willing to swap?

Here comes a tense time that usually turns out to be fun.

In a healthy marriage, almost without really thinking about it, the two parties are sensitive enough to each other's needs that they can meet those needs with some honest give and take. In dysfunctional marriages, and in marriages that have been damaged by crisis, this process of give and take falls apart. The exchange process is contaminated by resentment and unfinished business. Losses have not been brought to the open and grieved. Unfinished business, working under cover of ignorance or denial, works its mischief. Only when the other eight steps are successfully completed is the couple ready to negotiate some healthy give and take.

John, at first, was unwilling to give up his outside love interest. We insisted that interests of that sort outside the marriage bond be suspended first, before any further progress be considered. The fact that we consider such things immoral is important, but it does not pertain here. Issues of morality aside, distractions of that sort, which are already damaging the marriage bond, work counter to anything that would repair the bond. Gloria was just as stubborn. She clung to her depression; she'd had it so long it felt comfortable, like old slippers that have always been too big and flopped when she walked, but she was used to walking funny when they're on and she liked them.

Both persons had to make major concessions, and stick with them. Gloria had to agree to temporary medical intervention in her depression. She resisted the idea fiercely until we pressed upon her the damage her depression and a divorce would inflict upon people she loved. John was absolutely certain his new love could supply his needs and his present wife could not. We had to convince him to give reconciliation a chance.

Some clients actually write their demands and offers on pieces of paper and exchange them, much like mutual bargaining in union contract negotiations. Others keep it verbal. In this situation, oral contracts are to be honored at the same level as written ones. This is not quite the same as when you're hammering out a new marriage contract, though the same techniques apply. In this case, you are trying to correct a dysfunction right now, regardless of the passage you happen to be in or how far you've progressed in it.

Also, give and take may be necessary to prevent possible repetition of this particular crisis situation. Use the negotiation techniques you may know for contract-writing to reroute your marriage now.

Beverly and Larry's give-and-take session went something like this:

"I'll agree to work only a thirty-five hour work week. I will prepare our evening meal a couple of times a week," Larry said. "But I'd like some encouragement from you about my job performance."

Beverly admitted that she had been embarrassed to talk about Larry's work. "I know that I've stopped making any comments about it. I haven't known what to do. I thought talking about it—or giving superficial compliments—would only make it worse for you."

Now Larry could admit to himself and to Beverly, "As much as I resent the demotion, as much as I feel I could be doing so much more, I'm still very good at what I do. I need to have you tell me you know that too. And when I tell you about something I've done well, I still need you to say, 'I'm proud of you. I'm pulling for you.' "

Larry was also able to admit a hidden fear, which went something like this: "Since I am no longer the major bread-winner, I will lose control of the financial decisions. In fact, I will have little voice in how the money is spent."

Beverly could quickly dispel that fear. She had no problem with all major finances being a fifty-fifty decision, regardless of the proportions each of them brought in. She'd be happy to swap that for help around the house.

And back and forth they went, boosting each other, mending fences, building the future.

Step 9: Commit to Repairing the Future As Well As the Present

Part of this commitment includes committing as a team, not as two individuals after the same goal. Teamwork, in harness together, pulling as one.

Together you must address the major passages of your marriage where you're stuck. You must address the validity of true forgiveness in your lives. In this stage, you commit to mend what is flawed to date.

But there is more. You are also committing to repairs in the future. Once made rosy, no marriage remains that way. New hidden agendas, old ones incompletely vanquished, the tragic and comic operas of life, growing kids, and the changing nature of the marriage itself, all contribute to making it a new ball game. You are committing right now to work together on the problems these changes will generate.

Neither partner in a marriage can impose recovery upon the other person. No partner can rescue the spouse from a stuck spot. Like offering up prayer, it's something that must be done individually. The recovering partner can go only so far until and unless the other partner gets with the program. But one partner can do much. And two working in tandem can achieve phenomenal results.

We suggest that the spouses approach this activity much the way corporate executives work through their one-year, three-year, and five-year plans. The couple needs to talk about each of these time frames. Beverly admitted, for instance, that she enjoyed real estate and making her own money. She wanted to continue that for at least five or more years. Then together Larry and Beverly needed to work out a plan to accommodate her desire. In counseling we call this planning the "ongoing maintenance and repair" of the crisis.

Step 10: Minimize the Stressors in Your Marriage

This step is largely a matter of personal boundaries. Who invades? What invades? Church commitments, school commitments, service clubs, social clubs, committees, volunteer organizations, once-a-year things like the Fourth of July bash, or the home and garden show, or the fair, or the Christmas pageant.

Look at items one at a time. Christmas, for instance, is a big stress. How many Christmas cards do you send out and how tough is it to fulfill that self-imposed commitment? Can you get by with a few thousand fewer cookies and other baked goods this Christmas? How long does it take you to put up the decorations?

Everything mentioned above, and a hundred more categories, are important and worthwhile projects. But some of them have to go. You can't do it all. Just because it's a good idea doesn't mean you *have* to incorporate it into your life.

The bad news is, these items don't just splash down upon you. Even the healthiest marriages tend to revert back to earlier passages and more primitive coping mechanisms (nearly all of them unhealthy) when these stressors build to overload.

So list all the time-eaters and stressors in your marriage life. (For instance, because of his recent demotion, Larry felt a sense of economic insecurity. Yet he and Beverly had spoken of establishing a trust for their grandson's education. Once they did this, they might feel obligated to help the other grandchildren. This, then, became a major stressor for them.)

_____

_____

_____

_____

Now look at these stressors together. If time is one of your stressors, plan to cut back. "Hey, that won't be so easy!" some of our patients say.

And we quickly answer, "Of course it won't be easy. It's much easier to pick up another task than to say 'no,' and it's very hard to say 'no' if previously you said 'yes' to something. And you might be walking away from some important chores. You might ruffle some feathers on people who think you'd rather serve on the refreshment committee than spend a quiet night with your spouse, building intimacy and mutual pleasure."

In Larry and Beverly's case, some boundaries had to be set. If they wanted to give their grandson some assistance, how much would they give? They needed to set a specific amount that could be given to each grandchild without causing them any financial or emotional stress.

Plan to do this periodically—at least once a quarter—to nip overcommitment in the bud.

Surviving crises and resolving trauma builds a bond between two marriage partners. Something traumatic can actually foster a climate for intimacy. For a united front, a strong fortress wall, a strong marriage, is a formidable obstruction to a wrecking ball of stress and crises.

While you're working at that, you'll also want to examine closely the quality and quantity of marital intimacy and bonding.

Chapter 3

Is It Too Late to Establish Companionship and Unity?

R ob Millen, husband of Annie Warden Millen, had no intention of straying, really. At the church picnic he happened to notice Kerri. She wasn't wearing anything skimpy or revealing, but her shorts and top revealed nice legs and a well-shaped torso. She ended up just ahead of him in batting rotation at the softball game after lunch. They got to talking and she seemed sensible enough—not an airhead or anything. And yet there was a youthfulness about her, a verve and bounce that he enjoyed immensely. He was forty-nine and very tied down, she two decades younger and divorced. But then she went to bat and singled into right field and he struck out, so he didn't talk to her again that inning.

In the weeks that followed, Rob found himself thinking about Kerri a lot. She excited him. Annie didn't anymore. Kerri displayed the vigor and elan of youth. Annie marched purposefully through life with a frown on her face much of the time. And Annie, forty-seven, certainly didn't display any youth.

Annie didn't give him much time, either. She was always busy with something else. She was always too tired at night. She was always thinking about her schedule tomorrow, when Rob wasn't the least bit interested in what jobs loomed ahead. He wanted a little snuggling, a little sex right now. "Just a minute, dear. I need to make these phone calls." And she wasn't quite through menopause yet. Soon as that happened, she'd be a complete iceberg. An iceberg with crow's feet around her eyes.

Rob and Annie Millen needed to reestablish intimacy in their marriage or they were obviously headed for trouble. The second task of this passage—Renewing Love—is just that.

The Second Task: To Reestablish Intimacy

The primary task of this Fourth Passage is the intimacy of companionship and unity. An intimate relationship is just that—openly sharing your dreams, losses, hopes, fears, shames and joys with each other. Establishing a soul friendship with each other.

One of the best ways to foster intimacy is through acceptance of each other. Acceptance is the breeding ground for intimacy. It blots out hate. Carl and Bess Warden, married over four decades, would be the first to aver that commitment to your spouse means accepting both the good, the bad, the ugly, and the goofy about that person, the failures and inabilities as well as the glowing strong points. Real commitment and real intimacy are not based on a person's behavior, but on the promise we made before God to join with that person.

Debbie Newman further explains, "The purpose of creation was intimacy. God created us to be close to each other. He said it wasn't good for a man to be alone, even though he was in the Garden of Eden. He needed something, so God made woman. Human beings were meant to be intimate with each other.

"Intimacy goes wrong when we're ashamed and afraid to be close to someone else. We need it but we're afraid of it. We hide from one another and we also hide from God. We hide because we're afraid of what people will see in us—that we aren't worthy of their love."

Larry Crabb puts this into the following formula:

Fear of rejection = neurotic fear that we're not acceptable to our spouse, or to God.

Frankly, a lot of that fear is legitimate. We're fallen, we're human, we're not perfect. Yet, God accepts us as we are, unconditionally, and loves us for all our faults. We need to accept ourselves and to accept our spouses, imperfections and all.

There are two truths: One, there is a God; Two, you are not Him. Therefore, unconditional acceptance in its pure form is impossible for mortal beings. Whatever we mortal beings can do to strive for that, however, helps open up intimacy.

By this Fourth Passage, spouses have a pretty good idea, if not an excellent idea, of what their mate is like—his/her glaring faults, positive traits. To reestablish intimacy, you must each rejoice in the positive and accept the negative. Sometimes, merely a shift in emphasis, from what is wrong with each other to what is right, will open up a whole new avenue to an intimate relationship.

Along with *accept* we should stress the other "a" verb— *appreciate*. Don't just stop at accepting your mate and his/ her good and bad traits. Appreciate and celebrate the good traits, not just to each other, but to the world as well.

Larry and Beverly illustrate this. Larry, you'll remember, was demoted to a training position while Beverly's real estate career took off. Through counseling, Larry asked Beverly for some positive reinforcement of his work performance. Once she started doing that, Larry's self-image grew 100 percent.

Many psychologists believe that negative, tearing-down, derogatory messages are so powerful, so toxic, they can overpower positive messages by a ratio of three or four to one. That means that one negative comment can shoot down the good effects of three or four positive ones. To keep things in balance between the negatives and positives, the positive ones must outnumber the negatives by at least three to one. People don't realize that. And yet, what do you remember when someone evaluates your performance?

All the plaudits, or the one little negative thing the critic came up with?

We don't suggest that you lie. What do you see that's positive? This husband is an interested and involved father. That wife is a good listener. Whatever. But it must be true.

"Larry has so much experience, his company is tapping him to train the younger executives coming up in the firm." Beverly bragged one afternoon to her office mates.

"I think that's very wise," her office manager commented. "So many times we put older employees in a back office—out to pasture—and all that know-how and business savvy that only comes from years of experience goes right out the window."

Beverly took that comment to heart and made a conscious effort to restate it to Larry that evening. She could see Larry visibly swell with pride when she mentioned it.

Speaking of appreciation, when was the last time we appreciated what God has done for us? Hand in hand with appreciation of your marriage and your partner is appreciation of your God-given life. A daily prayer of gratitude would not ask God for anything but instead say, "Thank you."

There are other ways to reestablish intimacy than the ones we discussed above. Two of them get the most press: conflict and sex.

Conflict

Conflict is one of the best ways to build intimacy, yet it is usually the one most avoided or misused. We assume by about twenty-five years or so of marriage that you both have worked out control and conflict issues in your relationship. Thus, we will only briefly touch on this subject here. A formula you will see over and over again:

Two people living together = conflict.

Conflict leads either to separation or intimacy, depending upon how you deal with it. Separation doesn't have to be physical either. Many of our clients have separated emotionally from each other. They still live under the same roof, may even sleep in the same bed. Not quite strangers, but not intimate. They are separated. "Dry divorce," we call it.

Because conflict arises naturally, it should be neither encouraged nor avoided. It can become an opportunity for enhanced intimacy in this way: By deliberately practicing conflict resolution skills, two people get to know each other better and understand each other's innermost feelings. In fact, conflict resolution is so fundamental to a relationship that we could write a book on conflict rather than on marriage. It would serve the same purpose.

A detailed exposition of conflict resolution is included in our book, *Realistic Love* (Nashville: Thomas Nelson, 1993). For our purposes here, however, we will briefly outline these important principles. In order for these principles to work both of you must agree to stick to the rules!

1. Know Yourself.

In the midst of conflict, you must first understand what your position is, and why you hold to that position. You can discern this by examining your feelings. Do your feelings now resemble feelings you had while growing up?

Obviously, it is hard to be objective in the heat of an argument. So as a trial run, apply this principle, and the forthcoming principles, to a recent argument you had with your spouse. Analyze this former conflict and see if any fears or anger from your childhood influenced your behavior and feelings in this conflict.

2. Think.

Unless people are trained in the ability to look at alternatives and think, they can never resolve conflicts.

You must think about what your spouse's position really is. Remember the debating skills you may have learned or seen in high school? In order to understand your own position, you must thoroughly understand your opponent's position.

3. Avoid Absolutes.

Never speak in absolutes. Absolute statements usually

guarantee defensiveness because they're so overstated. Instead of absolutes, try to speak specifically on the issue that is bothering you.

Another trap to avoid is character assassinations or criticism. "You're so selfish, all you think about is yourself." How would you feel if someone was saying these things to you?

4. Stick to the Basics.

Keep to the issues being argued about. If the argument is about dirty laundry on the floor, keep that as the main issue. If it is about when a spouse is expected home at night, keep that the issue. It's easier said than done. Here's one tip to help you do it.

5. Keep Yourselves Out of the Fight.

"But how do we do that? We're the ones fighting?" you might protest.

Issues and persons are two different entities. Argue over the issues, but never allow your arguments to get personal. As much as you can, keep emotions out of it. When the need to win becomes so encompassing that it controls your emotions and thoughts, the disagreement then becomes a brutal dogfight, invariably shredding love and egos.

Dr. Frank Minirth defines a growing marriage as one that is increasing in conflict resolution skills. By this Fourth Passage, your conflict resolution skills should be as practiced as a trained mediator. However, if you suspect that conflict is still an issue in your marriage, we invite you to read the pertinent sections of *Realistic Love* (Nashville: Thomas Nelson, 1993) for an indepth review of the principles of conflict.

Sex

One of the best and most effective tools for building intimacy between a couple is through the special bonding that occurs within a sexual relationship.

At his forty-ninth birthday party, an over-the-hill roast, Rob Millen had received an important-looking paperback book with a tasteful, distinguished-looking cover, entitled *Sex and the Older Man*. All three hundred pages were blank.

Sex fosters intimacy, intimacy fosters sex, but they are not synonymous. Oneness in intercourse is an example of the soul oneness we hope to experience through intimacy. When a couple have been at it all these years, the sexual relationship easily slips into a benign dormancy.

The media does not help any. Nearly every ad, every self-help article, every TV show, and every film, suggests that sex is for the young. Face cream advertisements tell you to fight aging every step of the way. All the models in the catalogues are slim, even those modeling "older" fashions. Somewhere, somehow, you've been left out of life.

When you look in the mirror and decide a face lift would require a fork lift, when you pinch your spare tire and realize it would fit a road grader, you don't feel very sexy. And the people who know about such things all insist that it is attitude more than anything else that determines whether a man or woman radiates what is called "sex appeal." The first prerequisite for looking good to the opposite sex is a cheerful, upbeat feeling about yourself. That becomes increasingly difficult as age takes its toll on personal appearance and ability.

Then your twenty-year-old stares at you and exclaims, "Aw, come on, Pop! You don't still do *that*, do you?"

That . . . mumble, mumble . . . young whippersnapper! Humph!

The vivid, eager sexual dynamic you and your spouse enjoyed at the beginning of your marriage is probably a thing of the past. The young stud who handled several episodes a day has aged into the old stud who manages a couple a week . . . maybe. You will find some work involved in keeping your sexual union fresh and satisfying.

"But there is fun sex versus meaningful sex," explains Debi Newman. "Fun sex is the world's view of sex. The bedsheet-and-bare-shoulders episodes displayed on television and in the movies is made to look enticing and exciting.

The media portray different partners, no commitment—a relationship where pleasure is the only goal. It's all physical, all on the surface.

"By contrast, the sex that comes within the marital covenant is meaningful sex—where intimacy and pleasure are the goals—a special relationship with a particular person. Intimate marital sex provides an emotional intensity far greater than the physical orgasm—a soul orgasm if you will. Far too many of us are distracted by the world's view of fun sex. That's when our eyes tend to stray."

Rob Millen was also fighting another hidden enemy—misperception. Probably no area of life is more poorly perceived, and invites more just plain ignorance and stigma, as sex-over-forty. Even if you make that, sex-over-fifty myths and errors hold sway. Those untruths can ruin your sexual relationship and even open the partners to sexual dalliances with younger persons.

Sorting Fact from Fiction

True or false?

_____ Menopause does not actually affect women's sexual desires and performance.

_____ The first sign that the man has lost the capacity for sexual union is when he fails to achieve erection.

_____ Women over fifty eventually become sexually unresponsive.

_____ Talk and boasting aside, very few couples over forty-five engage in regular (weekly or more often) sex.

All the above are false, but the truth is more complex than a simplistic "true or false" permits. Knowing the facts can help you complete the overall goal of the Fourth Passage, to bond together in Renewing Love.

The Woman's Changes

Women have much to celebrate and to grieve.

"My goal is to have a baby in every decade," Mary Alice quips, only half-joking. With all her miscarriages, it's not a lighthearted issue. "This latest time, when I told people I was pregnant at the age of forty-one, they said, 'Oh, what a surprise!' No. Not a surprise.

"The last people we told about this latest pregnancy were my parents. We were afraid they'd get worried and upset because of my age and earlier difficulties. They were so supportive; they just kept on and on. 'You will get such pleasure from this baby,' they said. My mother told me how much her parents had enjoyed my uncle Jack, their seventh child. Uncle Jack went on to be a minister (not every child that comes along late in life will be wonderful like that, of course)."

Susanna Wesley's Charles, the eighteenth child in eighteen years of marriage, survived premature arrival, growing up to write a number of hymns we still sing, such as "O for a Thousand Tongues to Sing" and the Easter favorite, "Christ the Lord Is Risen Today."

But sooner or later, childbearing ends, for many women a bittersweet time. Technically, a woman enters menopause when her periods have ceased for a year. The median age is fifty, but individuals vary widely. The passing of her fertile years is something to grieve. Which is why we will touch on this subject again when we discuss grieving the loss of your youth in Chapter Five. Nothing tells a woman "Youth has fled" more forcefully than "You're too old to have babies."

And there is celebration too. No more fear of unintended pregnancy. No more monthly bloating and mess and unpredictable inconvenience. For most women, cessation of menses is Prometheus unbound. For many, their sexual enjoyment *increases* after menopause.

Not that menopause is a picnic in the park. As estrogen levels drop, tissues of the vulva and vagina may become thin and stiff, rendering intercourse painful. Lubricants may decrease, so a woman may have to apply a jelly or estrogen cream to this area before intercourse. And then there are the hot flashes. There may be some decline in the sex drive, but the loss is mild. Doctors have found that if a woman is sexually active before menopause she can continue sexual activity beyond menopause with fewer complications and problems than the woman who has been celibate or nearly so. Sexually active women don't undergo as much change. Many doctors recommend estrogen therapy not only to prevent the physical changes of menopause, but also to retard osteoporosis, that disease of advancing age in which a woman's bones become bent and brittle.

The sex act itself changes somewhat. We divide the sexual episode into four phases: Desire, Excitement, Orgasm, and Resolution. The first phase, Desire, begins with thoughts of the spouse. During the next phase, Excitement, the skin flushes. The man's scrotum and testicles shift. His penis rises to erection. So does her clitoris, as she releases a slippery, wet lubricant.

The sexual experience levels out now, which is actually a part of the excitement phase. Unless he prolongs it, a man's plateau can be extremely short. The woman's progress ambles across a relatively long plateau of some minutes.

Then man and woman arrive at Orgasm. He achieves ejaculation. She experiences a thrilling tingle of pleasure rippling across her. Man and woman need not reach the top simultaneously; they do have different experiences.

In the Fourth Passage the woman's arousal graph alters shape. It takes her somewhat longer during the excitement and plateau phases to build to orgasm, and the orgasm itself is shorter. Resolution, the final phase, happens more quickly. But it's all still there, all still giving pleasure, and as far as medical findings reveal, a woman may continue to enjoy the special intimacy of sex until her dying day.

Pause here to list some of the old wives' tales you grew up with, such as "a woman is not interested in sex after fifty."

How do these assumptions stack up against the medical
knowledge we just summarized?

1. _____

2. _____

3. _____

4. _____

The Man's Changes

Rob Millen didn't see any change in his own sexual responses. After all, he wasn't *that* old. If during sex he was a
little slower getting started, and it wasn't quite as wild and
satisfying as it used to be, that was Annie's fault, not his. If
he had a sexual partner like Annie used to be, he'd perform
like he did in the beginning.

Rob Millen was talking himself into sexual self-destruc-
tion.

Says Robert Hemfelt, "This Fourth Passage is an extremely vulnerable time for affairs. The line of thought goes
I want to know if I'm still lovable. Most commonly, though,
that thought lies below conscious level. The person becomes
insatiably attracted to a neighbor or a fellow employee. It
feels like true love or intense romance. Actually, it's a part of
that person that's questioning his or her worth in other areas
of life. Seeking out a romantic partner provides a strong
counterfeit validation of personal identity. 'I am loved for
me.' "

An affair, whether overtly sexual or only emotional, can
also provide counterfeit validation or confirmation of youth
not yet completely lost. To the persons involved, it seems so
straightforward—we have found new love again—when it is
actually born not of love or even physical attraction but of
vague, unspoken inner needs having nothing at all to do
with that enchanting other person.

"The man who understands the changes old age brings
and adjusts to them," says Dr. Minirth, "will continue to
enjoy sexual expression long into old age. The men who
refuse to recognize the changes, or blame them on outside

influences such as their wives or illness—imagined illness or real illness, either one . . . they're going to lose their capacity for sexual expression. And that is so unfortunate. You have to be flexible."

What changes can truly be laid at the door of advancing age? Again, let's use fifty as the average age when changes begin to manifest themselves. The man will benefit from longer foreplay. He doesn't achieve erection as quickly, and it may be less firm than it used to be. His orgasm, too, will be shorter and may peak earlier than in the past. His resolution time will certainly be shorter—perhaps seconds instead of minutes. A longer time will elapse before he can begin sexual activity again. Against these losses, he will find considerable gain: He can sustain erections longer and will probably have better control. Thus, the sexual experience can be even more satisfying for both partners.

Some problems are medical. Diabetes, prostate problems or surgery, hardening of the arteries, and some types of neurological disorders like arthritis of the back, which can affect the sacral nerves, sometimes reduce a man's sexual desire. Men at risk for heart attack, or who have recently survived a heart attack, may develop a fear of dying during intercourse. As a result they abstain. Such cases are extremely rare, and when they occur, there are almost always other factors involved. Sexual activity is actually good exercise, with intercourse equivalent to climbing a flight or two of stairs.

Certain prescription drugs for heart problems, however, such as blood thinners, can reduce or destroy the man's capacity to make love. Betablockers can reduce desire. Consult your doctor if these drugs are causing difficulty. Other options may be available to you.

Simply increasing a man's level of exercise can raise libido. That's equally true for women.

List five myths you've heard of that cause sexual slowdown in middle-aged men (whether you have arrived at that age yet or not).

1. _____
2. _____
3. _____
4. _____
5. _____

Adjusting to the Changes

Now that you know a little something about the changes you can expect in each other, go back to each list you made —the ones listing reasons for sexual slowdowns for a man and for a woman over fifty. For each item on those lists name at least two ways to adjust in order to minimize or negate each reason for sexual slowdown. Can't come up with many? Then let's look at some suggested adjustments others have found.

Advisors and counselors recommend these points to adjust to the sexual changes of the Fourth Passage.

Time

Since both man and woman require more time to achieve maximum pleasure, relax. Don't rush. Take more time. Also, observe what time of day seems to produce the most satisfying results. Late at night is usually the least satisfying time, and yet it's often the only time available. Experiment, if possible, with midday episodes, perhaps a marital nap before dinner, or early morning activity. The added benefit of having children out of the house during this passage is that you both have the freedom to make love at any time of the day.

What times work the best for you? What pleases you both the most? The newness of varying the time also increases pleasure.

Other factors

Know what your prescription medicines do. Ask questions. Understand that alcohol, stress, worry, and fatigue work against you now even more than when you were younger. If estrogen therapy from a gynecologist, or surgical aids provided by a urologist, seem indicated, explore their possibility. Hearing aids and eyeglasses compensate for the losses of age. Why stop there?

Talk

You've been together so long you each know what the other likes, right? Don't be so sure. Annie and Rob hadn't mentioned a word about sexual techniques or preferences in twenty years. Each harbored secret longings and desires, for different positions, different situations, new techniques. Rob liked to think that a few interesting experiments would restore some of the fun, but he never said so out loud. He couldn't stand the thought of being laughed at.

Don't assume your partner believes such-and-so, or would never consider so-and-so. Ask. "Do you want to do this? Do you want to try that? How can I help you?" Experiment with new ways and new techniques.

Dr. Hemfelt points out three levels of communication in sex. First is the physical act itself, a powerful form of communication. Second is talking about sex, setting boundaries and priorities, explaining needs. The third is talking about talking about sex.

Often we hear this dialogue in counseling sessions:

"Every time I want to talk about sex," he complains, "you seem to get angry and tense."

She responds, "That's because every time we bring up the subject, you adopt this accusing tone of voice that suggests I'm not giving you what you want."

They are talking about how they talk about sex. That is actually very important, because you'll notice in the dialogue above that there were misconceptions on both sides. Once those misconceptions are worked out, by talking, sharing sexual needs with one another will be much easier.

Make contact

People of all ages, but older people especially, over and over again tell us, "I just want the closeness. I want to be held. To snuggle. Sure, sex is great. But physical closeness is great, too, whether it ends up as sex or not." Hold each other. Hug. That simple thing is immensely reassuring and satisfying.

In fact, non-sexual physical contact is actually a need no matter what passage of marriage a couple is in. You'd be surprised how many men in our counsel say, "Sometimes all I really want to do is hold my wife without the pressure of it leading to sex."

Watch out for your self-talk

Your body has, perhaps, been sagging for years, picking up a few more pounds, altering with age. But you didn't notice it before, really; you were too busy. Suddenly, here in mid-life, the flaws all jump off the mirror at you. What a frump! Who could love *that*! It sure ain't what it used to be. Recognize these negative images for what they are—distortions. You're experiencing sticker shock, the same as a person out to buy a new car who hasn't been shopping for cars in a while. The change sneaked up on you.

Too many people resign from sexual activity, or even from life itself (not physically, but emotionally) because of what they think they see in the mirror. Physical appearance is secondary to true sexual attraction; film casting directors all agree on that point. It's the personality, the chemistry, that makes a person sexually desirable.

Pops and Granny, fresh from rural Pennsylvania, got off the airplane in Las Vegas, their first visit there. Culture shock. Pops watched the girls intently, lithe and supple girls leaving planes and getting on them, playing the slots, working the gate desks. Granny watched Pops, and she was not amused. Neither was she worried. To her grandson she commented, "He's harmless."

Intergenerational family message or cultural myth, she and Pops were both buying into the notion that sex ends in later life. Don't you accept any old wives' tales. Family and cultural myths are just that—myths—and enjoy no support from fact.

Rekindle romance

Rob Millen didn't realize it, but Annie also felt estrangement in this Fourth Passage. Once she got Beth Anne married, Annie felt lost—at loose ends—as we mentioned at the beginning of this book. The fuel for her train—making the wedding arrangements—had run out. Now what? Her husband steamed along on his own track, leaving her to hers. And her train had stalled.

Annie, too, had seriously considered just hanging it up. She'd be neither more nor less happy apart from Rob than with him. She could travel, do things. For once in her life she could march to her own drummer. Tempting! So tempting.

But . . .

But . . . there was the commitment she had made aeons ago at the wedding altar, just as Beth Anne had, just as her parents had before her.

But . . . there was the example she and Rob set for Beth Anne and nieces and nephews and future grandchildren. Whether consciously or not, the younger generation looked to them as models.

Those buts were important.

But! She would not continue like this. She would not spend the rest of her days in this emotional vacuum. Either her marriage would again become an important element in her life, or she was going to leave.

Most reluctantly, because the temptation to freedom glowed so brightly, she decided to make a stab at turning her marriage around at this late date.

But how?

She got her first notion when she arrived early for a church bazaar committee meeting at Joan's. Now Joan was not nearly so slim as Annie, and unlike Annie eschewed hairdressers. To an objective observer, Annie was much more attractive for her age than was Joan. And yet, Joan seemed to have an emotionally satisfying marriage. An emotionally satisfying everything, actually.

Joan yelled, "Come in!" when Annie knocked at her door.

Annie stepped inside. She would have said, "I'm sorry; I may be a little early," but Joan was on the phone. She was making weekend reservations at a bed and breakfast up on the lake.

Joan completed the business and hung up. "Coffee's on the stove. I'm glad you dropped by early. Can you help put out the sticky buns?"

"Certainly!" Annie popped open the microwave and slipped the buns out onto a platter. "So you're going up to that B & B. I've heard of that place. They say it's very romantic. You and your husband?"

"Yep." Joan's eyes twinkled. "To keep the house warm, every now and then you gotta throw another log on the fire."

We suggest now that you rethink and revitalize your romantic love life if need be.

And you wag your head sadly. "You don't know my spouse. Everything is cast in cement. We always did it this way, and we're always going to do it this way. You can't imagine the lockstep my mate has settled into in midlife. We're in a deep rut."

We certainly do understand. We see it constantly in counseling. You are not alone. But remember the rules of contract negotiation, tennis, and life. When one person changes, the other cannot remain unchanged. The other must adjust.

In Annie's case, Rob had plateaued at work, even though he considered himself indispensable. He worked a sixty-hour week simply because he'd been putting in extra time ever since he started there. Annie couldn't see that he had anything to prove to anyone. She resented all that time he lavished on his dead-end job. And Annie didn't even know about Rob's attraction to Kerri.

We urge you to be creative about rejuvenating your sexual

union. Look at new ways you can jumpstart your relationship. If you were in Annie's position (and you just might be, if you are in the Fourth Passage), what are some creative ways you might redirect your husband's energies and interests to better support his marriage? There are several ways to approach the problem.

Some years ago, a film actress claimed that her actor husband's obsession with watching newscasts was damaging their time together—wrecking the evening meal, playing havoc with schedules. He had to see them *all* (this was before twenty-four-hour cable news and VCRs). Frustrated, she emphasized her complaint by draping herself across their TV set, wearing only a rose in her teeth. We are not necessarily recommending that, but it's certainly creative.

Annie was more direct. She unplugged the TV set and cut the plug off. She made an appointment with Rob's secretary at work for an hour of his time. She showed up at his office door one lunch time with a picnic basket—he had been planning to work through lunch. From Joan she got the phone number for that bed and breakfast.

She fumed and cajoled and she laid it all out for Rob. "If you want this marriage to survive, you're going to have to start taking an interest in it."

We do not necessarily recommend confrontation of that sort, either. Remember, threats of that sort are one of the sex killers. In Annie's case, it was the only way she could capture Rob's attention. Most important, she was not bluffing. She really was convinced that she had reached the end of her rope. But, also importantly, she did not dump it completely onto Rob. She took positive steps and urged him to join her.

Finally Annie used a powerful bond to strengthen their sexual intimacy: the bond of a shared history. That, too, will help you renew your love during the Fourth Passage.

The Bond of a Shared History

A few years ago at the annual Old-Timer's Day in Mount Rainier National Park, a ranger in his eighties pointed to a faint stain by the huge fireplace at Paradise Inn. "That's bear grease from the winter of '22," he explained. "Bad snow year. Then during a thaw, but while the snow was really deep yet, a few of the black bears came out of hibernation early. Made a major nuisance of themselves around the residential area and the inn here. We ended up shooting one. It was illegal, so we decided to burn him in the fireplace here. He didn't burn worth zip. All he did was render down to gallons of grease. It came running out of the fireplace, seeping into the floor boards. What a mess."

And the other old-timers nodded, smiling.

Memories

As the avocado is to guacamole, so is laughter to your family history. When you laugh, you feel good literally. Contrary to the physical effects anger promotes, which we discussed in the last chapter, laughter works on your body much the same way a tranquilizer does. Without getting too involved in our explanation, laughter produces endorphins which relieve pain and create pleasure sensations.

Many laugh-provoking incidents will involve the children in some way, but equally important is the history of the two of you with all its quirks and nuances.

The past calls every person strongly. Times were different then, and life seemed closer to the edge. And so people put together reunions—reunions of armed forces units, or old-timers, or the survivors of a momentous event. They get together to share the memories, to keep alive the history.

Your marriage has just that sort of animated history. It includes things not funny at the time but fun now in retrospect. You survived some dreadful (or just dreadfully weird) crises. That's an important bond, no less powerful than the bond that draws old-timers and classmates from hundreds and even thousands of miles away.

Many people will reminisce about anything else but the marriage itself—kids, the cat, the grandkids. Physical ailments get a lot of play. The marriage itself and the memories it generates, get hardly any play. To put the power of that bond to use, emphasize your marital history. Talk about it. Relive it.

Susan Hemfelt explains about using memories to bond. "We spent our honeymoon at Estes Park in the cabin Granddad built. It's always been an important place in my life. I remember when I was in the ninth grade, sitting on a rock, thinking, 'This is as close to heaven as you can get without being there.' What a magnificent confirmation of the magnitude of God's creation!

"The place grew on Robert also. It means something to him as well. We try to go up there every year. Now the fourth generation goes there. That little house is the locus of so much family history, and ninety-nine percent of it is good history. There's barely enough water; it's rustic; it forces you to take your mind off the frills of life, and get to basics."

She pauses thoughtfully. "It's a lot of work for Mother. The bugs are a nuisance, but not too bad. They're supposed to be there.

"We all went up there for Christmas in 1983. My brother-in-law changed the alternator in my dad's car; it was sixteen degrees below zero. The kitchen was so cold the turkey wouldn't bake. My father and brother-in-law tried to seal the cabin with plastic sheets. They got the temperature to rise a bit; it was thirty-five degrees in the kitchen. Mom cooked Christmas dinner in thermals. Later we had T-shirts printed with 'I survived Christmas '83.'

"There's always such a water shortage, we don't flush for everything. But you see, that cabin doesn't just have a history of a string of strange anecdotes. It has a deeper history, of all the people working together solving problems, such as ways to conserve water."

A rich heritage, threaded through four generations. The Hemfelt children are embraced in history, just as the Hemfelt marriage is.

Think about the memories that can bind and renew your marriage. What strange and tragic and delightful and unique things happened in your marriage?

What do your children and spouse know about your youth? Note at least two things that you would want them to remember:

_____

_____

How about your and your spouse's ancestors? _____

_____

_____

You probably have some colorful characters in your family. What stories of these legends would you want to tell your kids?

_____

_____

. . . to your spouse?

_____

_____

What do your children know about the early years of your marriage, before they were here (like the times you just took off for a weekend together in the city or for a special day at the shore)?

_____

_____

What memories do you have of:
    —the birth of your first child?
    —your first house?
    —a special family vacation?
    —graduation of a child from high school? From college?

Stitched together, all these patches of recollections form an enchanting crazy-quilt of history.

"Okay," said Annie, "so exactly where and how do I reinforce our trove of memories? Our history?"

The dinner table is an excellent place to begin. Annie Millen never let TV get in the way of dinner again. She and Rob sat at the table and conversed during dinner—always. (If some family member simply cannot be weaned away from evening news, use a VCR; let him or her watch the news after dinner. It won't get *that* stale in half an hour.) The dinner table is a good laughing place, one of those warm and comfortable places where the family knows it can feel bright and goofy.

Look for small things to celebrate: getting the dog's teeth cleaned; changing the ribbon in your typewriter; the victory of Dad who's been trying to improve his language at work, making it clear through the day without a single unseemly word; finishing the drywall in the basement . . . there are lots of things.

Play games together. Friends of ours play three games of backgammon after dinner. It doesn't happen every single night because other things intrude. Sometimes they're not together, or they have company. The person who's behind at the end of each month buys dinner out for the other.

Record your history. Write a letter to each other on every anniversary. Take videos or photographs of both special events and also the everyday. In every historical collection, the most valuable and telling photos are not of the prominent people standing around shaking hands, but of ordinary folk in ordinary situations. That's why the television program, *Funniest Home Videos*, struck so many chords. It's the same with your family.

Most of all, examine your family traditions. We are a tradition-bound people, all of us, and our traditions in large measure define us.

Traditions

A friend of ours speaks lovingly of her own family's tradition: "It's Christmas Eve. The same every year. Mom works herself to death in the kitchen making this elaborate Scandinavian lutefisk feast."

"Lutefisk? Isn't that some sort of fish?"

"It sure is. And does it *smell.* I said 'Dad, the Swedes didn't eat this stuff because it was festive. It was the middle of winter and all they had was cured cod to eat.' "

"But you eat it anyway."

" 'It's tradition.' Dad answers. Then he puts on his crazy Viking helmet."

"With horns?"

"Yeah. And we sing the songs about how bad lutefisk smells. And we tell the limericks. Tradition. Crazy, but we love it. The dinner is so famous we get more friends and family every year."

Tradition. A crazy time-honored tradition that is passed on from generation to generation. A wonderful and very effective bonding tool.

Akin to memories are the traditions of your family and the ancestors before you. The culturally conservative Navajo understands that away from his land and his traditions, he cannot truly be Navajo. Not just his traditions shape his identity; his practice of them maintains it. Some people, such as the European immigrants who flocked to America in the early 1900s, tried to put the Old Country behind them, only to find themselves and their children becoming emotionally impoverished. History and traditions kept the Jewish race intact through two thousand years of dispersal and persecution. Today, they occupy the ancestral land, speaking a pure tongue that, logically speaking, should have died long ago.

Traditions have that same preserving and bonding power for your family. They will define your family just as powerfully as they define clans and nations everywhere.

Traditions vary from "What we do every Christmas" to "Whether we use cloth napkins at the dinner table." Make certain you savor the traditions that mark you apart as a couple. Celebrate them. Enjoy them. And be sure to pass your family traditions along to your grandchildren.

For Every Hello There Is a Good-bye

Your relationship is growing, expanding, opening up to new frontiers. You're exploring a new realm together as you expand and reestablish your intimacy with each other. That's the hello. To make way for these new frontiers, you must leave others behind. That's the good-bye.

Chapter 4

Good-bye to Your Parents

*I*n a space of three years, Robert Hemfelt lost both parents and Frank Minirth lost his mother. Frank's father was gravely ill. The prior generation is leaving, and their leaving wreaks havoc on the children as much as on themselves.

Take for example a woman in her fifties whom we'll call Ella. Neither of Ella's parents can bring themselves to accept death. For poor Ella, it's worse than watching a torture chamber because she's getting sucked into it. As death draws closer, those two people, terrified of losing each other, terrified of death, cling piteously to each other and to Ella. They cannot bear to think of temporary separation, let alone terminal separation. No matter how frequently Ella visits or how much she does, it's not enough.

Ella herself is going to have immense difficulty coming to terms with her own mortality because her parents' fear of death—a major piece of unfinished business—is descending upon her head. In counseling we can help Ella accept her limitations and grieve them. We can help her gain hope in Christ and a measure of peace. But then she goes home to Mom and Dad.

In contrast, if the later Fifth Passage goes well, the passage Ella's mom and dad are now in, husband and wife forge strong spiritual ties with each other and with God (we will talk about those ties in *Transcendent Love* (Nashville: Thomas Nelson, 1993), our fifth book, touching on that passage). These ties, however, do not bind and cling. Filled with shared strength, husband and wife can easier make peace with reality, enjoy what years or hours they have left, and then let go.

Ella is stuck in the Fourth Passage with her marriage and the Fifth Passage with her parents', and she isn't unique. The next task of the Fourth Passage is to grieve the losses characteristic of these years.

The Third Task: To Grieve the Particular Losses of This Passage

Life is full of losses, and part of the successful completion of each passage is to come to terms with the inevitable losses of that passage. That means grieving them through and looking for the unseen blessings they often bring.

The apostle Paul suffered from the slings and arrows of life as much as any person in the Bible: shipwrecks, mob violence and persecution, and imprisonment. Yet he could tell the Roman Christians, "All things work together for good to those who love God, to those who are the called according to His purpose" (Rom 8:28).

Put another way: life is full of ups and downs, peaks and valleys. If it weren't for the valleys, we'd never appreciate the peaks; we'd be living on one long boring plain. We like to tell our patients that each good-bye (or loss) has a corresponding hello (or blessing).

A fact of life most often avoided is that we are all leaving eventually. We will all die. Some of us are just crossing that line sooner than others.

A lot of losses hit at once during this Fourth Passage— your parents, your jobs, your kids, your health, your youth, and some of your dreams. Along with those losses come just

as many gains and joys if they are recognized and grabbed
when they happen.

We will discuss the first and most profound loss—the one
of your parents in this chapter. Subsequent chapters will
cover the other losses. The way you accomplish the third
task of this Fourth Passage is in how you handle and cope
with these losses and embrace the corresponding hellos that
come with them.

Changing Roles

The Fourth Passage marks a sandwich period for many
couples. Children and parents both rely on you for psychological and practical support. You are being squeezed from
both angles by the separate generations. Suddenly you are
the responsible one to take care of and advise both generations. There seems nowhere to go for your support—the
buck stops here.

This is why we stress the support you each must provide
the other as you shoulder these immense burdens. And,
don't forget God. For most of your lives you have looked to
your parents as demi-gods. If you accomplished the tasks of
the Third Passage successfully, you took them off this pedes-
tal and put them on your level. Now they look to you as a
demi-god and so do your children. This is an overwhelming
responsibility.

The person most capable to handle that responsibility is
God. He is, after all, the real God. And, the real one does a
much better job than a demi-god. Daily meditation helps
much to accomplish this purpose. A close relationship with
God, as is very plausible at this stage of your life, opens up
communication for you to receive guidance on the very issues your children or parents may saddle you with.

A close relationship with each other—intimate, as we
mentioned in the last chapter—also helps the communication. God uses just about everyone in our lives to communi-
cate with us. Your spouse is the one closest to you and may
have the privilege of being a pipeline for God's messages.

A very real hello, joy if you will, in this passage as you say good-bye and grieve the losses, is the enhanced relationship (closeness) with God and with your spouse. It is a common joy and hello through all losses inherent in this stage of your life. Embrace it with vigor.

Encompass More of God

Doris, a client of ours, followed her heart and defied her father's wishes, marrying a musician. Doris' daddy was wealthy. He could not approve of Doris' husband who dropped out of college to follow his music. Despite that her husband beat the odds and made a reasonable living as a pianist, relations between Doris and her daddy remained cold and restrained from the engagement right up to his death.

With his passing, during Doris' Fourth Passage of marriage, she found herself in a profound spiritual crisis. The God of her prior Christian convictions appeared to be far too unfair and vengeful to warrant worship. She dwelt to the point of obsession, on the tragedies that struck believers and unbelievers. She could not be reconciled to them. Because her crisis of faith coincided closely with her father's death, her pastoral counselor sent her to us.

To make a long therapy story short, Doris figured out that the death of her father had triggered within her the memories of all that pain she felt when her human father rejected her. She had projected the pain and injustice together upon her heavenly Father. Only after she grieved all that pain out, and released it, could she come back and embrace her heavenly Father. And embrace Him she did, more profoundly than ever she had known Him before.

Unresolved issues can and do spill over into the Fourth Passage, or wherever they are triggered by some event. And they can bar union with God just as easily as they bar intimacy with your spouse. If you have trouble reaching new depths of one-ness and understanding with God, look to your past for clues. Is something back there damaging your faith now?

Carl Jung claimed you do not come to a true mature spiritual acceptance of God until the second half of life. Now, in these later passages, you can get down to the deepest levels of spiritual insight. There are two archaic and distorted views of God you may have to dismiss first. One is Santa Claus God, who can supply the grocery list of needs you present Him in prayer. The second is the harsh and vengeful Scorekeeper God, who's planning to punish you for all those wrongs. Both are supported by selected Scripture verses. Neither represents the true God when all Scripture is viewed.

How much of your past is coloring your view of God now? First, what are your human father's (or adoptive father's) attributes, good or bad; is (was) he domineering? Authoritarian? A marshmallow? Tender? Cold? Silly? Practical? List his ways:

1. _____
2. _____
3. _____
4. _____

Next, what are your mother's?

1. _____
2. _____
3. _____
4. _____

Now, what are God's attributes as you see them?

1. _____
2. _____
3. _____
4. _____

Compare the lists. Either your parents do indeed reflect the heavenly Father—and many do, because that's what parents are supposed to do according to divine plan—or you are projecting your earthly parents upon the heavenly one. Even more likely, you are only coloring your view of God in a limited way by your memories of your parents. Give the point as much thought as possible. Lord willing, it will lead to deeper insight.

We recommend saying good-bye in emotional and mental terms to your parents before you have to practically—before they leave this earthly plane.

Lost Parents

Gerald and his wife came in for counseling when Gerald's father was diagnosed with cancer. They thought the core of their problems was their marriage relationship. After one or two sessions, we suspected differently. We asked Gerald, "How do you feel about your father's pending death?"

"It's tough, but I just have to face it," he answered.

As he answered a few more questions in that vein, we picked up undercurrents of denial, so we pushed him to talk about his relationship with his dad. Slowly the pattern emerged.

"My dad was in control," Gerald said. "We all jumped when he told us to do something." And he described one day when his seven-year-old brother knocked over his mom's favorite lamp because he responded to one of dad's commands too quickly.

We asked Gerald, "Describe some close moments with your father that you remember."

"Well, uh . . . I don't quite understand the question."

"You know; times when he got down on all fours and played with you. Took you in his lap to read."

Minutes passed. Tears welled in his eyes as he admitted, "None I can remember." Instead, he described the times he yearned for a hug or an "I'm really proud of you" from his father, times that never came.

Gerald was having trouble saying good-bye to his father because he had never said hello to him. Their relationship resembled the interaction between a sergeant and a private, not a father and a son. His father's imminent death triggered the time-release capsule of the lack of a loving relationship.

The death of a parent (or the debilitation of a parent through disease or senility) is a powerful transition. You left home and said good-by residentially to your parents in the First Passage of marriage, after the wedding.

Yet the ultimate good-bye doesn't come, for most of us, until the parent begins to crumble physically or mentally. Unconsciously we think, *This is the person who brought me into this world. This is the person who nurtured me in my early years. I'm losing a part of me.* Even if you've said good-bye to your parents in earlier passages, they still represent the ultimate security symbol for you. You still view them as flawed-though-godlike figures. And you still, as Gerald did, mourn any lack in your relationship.

Saying Good-bye

We suggest that you say good-bye to your parents now. If you are adopted or grew up in foster care, you have several sets of parents to think about. Two possible situations pertain here as you say this good-bye. In the first, your parents are still living, perhaps still very much a part of your lives. The second occurs when your parents are deceased or beyond contact, perhaps so debilitated by a stroke or Alzheimer's or other ailment, they are not available to you consciously. Fortunately, it's never too late to say good-bye.

Parents Who Are Still Here

We suggest writing a letter to each parent, telling of the high points and not-so-high points of your life growing up under his/her care and guidance. Remember, this letter is for your private growth. You may choose never to show the letter to your parents. Use your discretion.

With a few words each to remind you of the memories, list some good times. Treat the items separately, for each has touched you uniquely.

1._____

2._____

3._____

Now list the bad times with your parent. The bitter as well as the sweet. Both must be recognized.

1. _____
2. _____
3. _____

List some memorable gifts from your parents. They could be material, such as a bike or O-scale locomotive, or non-material gifts such as a camping experience, or a week in the country.

1. _____
2. _____
3. _____
4. _____

Are there other things about your parents that stand out?

_____

_____

Now celebrate and grieve each item appropriately. Use the grieving process we discussed in Chapter Two to fully grieve and resolve each item you listed above. Pay particular attention to those items under the bad times. If they are still fresh in your memory after so many years away from living under your parents' roof (or perhaps they happened only recently), they can be clues to time-release capsules that will affect you now or in the future.

Consider grieving the good times, too. The sad part is that they will never happen again. Perhaps they were not as good as they should have been.

An added benefit to handling the loss of your parents properly is that you will be preparing your children to also handle your leaving appropriately. Remember Ella at the beginning of this chapter? She was not getting a good example from her parents on impending death. But, through her therapy, she was stopping that unfinished business from being passed onto her children.

How About You?

Take a moment to reflect upon your view of death. How much of it is colored by your parents? Do you remember how they handled their parents' passing (if your grandparents are no longer living)? Check the following statements to see what example your parents set for you:

_____ In my family, death was never discussed. We avoided the subject whenever possible.

_____ The passing of my grandparent(s) was a terrible burden on my parent(s). The last few months of their life was torture for them and for my parents. I felt that my grandparent(s) was/were afraid of dying and clung inappropriately to my parent(s).

_____ I was never involved in death of relatives during my childhood. My parents felt it was necessary to shield me from these experiences.

_____ I can count on one hand the number of times my family spoke of death or dying.

If you could check more than a few of these statements, you probably did not get an education on coping with death in your family-of-origin. You may have an even more difficult time coming to terms with your parents' deaths. Relying on your religious beliefs and study can help amend this lack of education.

By contrast, peruse the following statements to see if you were given a different lesson on dying:

_____ In my family we discussed death whenever the subject arose.

_____ Even a pet's death was grieved and dealt with as a family unit.

_____ My parents were compassionate and loving during my grandparents' (or other important relative's) passing.

_____ I remember there was a peace, a special relationship between them that I enjoyed being around.

_____ I know that death is not an ending but a beginning of another, totally new relationship with God.

You will be passing a beneficial legacy on to your children if you grieve the loss of your parents' relationship and say good-bye to them successfully. Also, you will set an example for your children, perhaps give them the opportunity to say good-bye to you as a parent and hello to you as a friend.

Back to your letter. Now, capitalize on the good times with your parents that you listed. Then tell of some values of your parents that you've adopted in your own life—how you admire their leadership and its role in shaping your life. Reinforce your undying love for them and admiration—strengthen that emotional bond. Forgive your parents for any of the bad times, at the same time purging any resentment and bitterness you carry against them. Finally say good-bye to the role you know them in—the guiding and all-knowing parent—and say hello to them as a friend, peer.

Rework the letter over and over until you are satisfied with the results. If you feel it would be beneficial, pick a special time and place and give it to each parent.

You may choose to do this together with both parents or separately. Whatever feels right to you is the best way.

This will be something entirely new for your folks, so be empathetic and sensitive. Assure them you aren't leaving them alone. Rather you are embracing a new and very special relationship with them.

It may take a while, especially if you're in frequent contact with them. And, they may not exactly warm up to the notion of being your equal, either. The fact that you are probably now older than they were when they married doesn't enter into it a bit. Again, remember the rules of the game: if one person changes, the other has to adjust in some way. If you change the way you relate to your parents, they will have to change the way they relate to you.

If your parents are distant (geographically or emotionally) but still alive and well, you may be able to establish a better relationship with them now. We've found that patients who try to build or improve a comfortable relationship with parents, whether they actually achieve it or not, can handle their parents' deaths reasonably well. Those who run from the anger and pain, who avoid contact or let sour memories prevail, tend to crumble when the separation is cemented by death.

If Your Parents Are Gone

If your parents are either deceased or physically unavailable for some reason, follow the same process we discussed above. Further, if you are an adoptee, you may know your adoptive parents, but not your biological ones. Use this same process to say good-bye both to your adoptive parents and to your biological parents.

Write each deceased or unavailable parent a letter or record a cassette tape. Once you've reworked each letter to cover all the points you want to make, picture that person in your mind. You've no picture to make? The parent was removed from your life before the memories began? Then you will essentially say good-bye to your concept of that parent, the imagined pictures in your mind. That's fine. Obviously, since a deceased or absent parent cannot know what you're doing, all this is for your benefit. Your perceptions of that unavailable parent are what you are saying good-bye to.

Use the letter as a tangible object in lieu of the persons themselves. Touch it. Look at it.

In your prayers to God on behalf of that parent, give thanks for the influence the person played in your life, if only peripherally. Even bad influences are not all bad. The most destructive influence still shapes you in some positive way and makes you what you are.

For example, a woman now in our counsel suffered serious child abuse and neglect. She is thankfully working through her pain in therapy. However, she is a caring and involved parent as a result of that bad influence. "I vowed *never* to do to my children what my parents did to me," she declared. She was on the verge of breaking her vow; old patterns are almost impossible to shake. Her children's welfare drove her into counseling and therapy. She and her children all benefitted from a tragic experience (though not experiencing the tragedy at all would have been vastly better!).

Now, finally, picture in your mind's eye waving good-bye to that parent and walking away from them. Even if a parent is senile or comatose or unreceptive, you can say hello and good-bye to him or her with a monologue or a letter. In the movie *Five Easy Pieces,* Jack Nicholson returned home to say good-bye to a dad who had suffered a stroke. He wheeled the old man, who was unable to speak or move, into a field —acres and acres of blue sky and waving cornstalks—and knelt beside him. His conversation with the stonefaced old man went something like this:

"I have no idea if you are in there or not. I have no idea if you can hear me. But I have to tell you why I haven't been back in years." And then the painful memories flowed.

In that monologue, Nicholson was both saying good-bye and hello. Often, saying good-bye can best be done by first saying hello. By talking through their past, the son was able to begin to establish some kind of relationship with the old man.

Failing to say good-bye to your parents with heart as well as mind is a sure way to get stuck in this passage. As Susan Hemfelt says, "You can't get anywhere focusing on the now and the past. You have to focus on the now and the future."

When the Good-Byes Don't Happen

He's been so frequently used as the subject of movies, books and plays, he's a stereotype: He's the forty-something guy who flushes his marriage, his job, his family—everything you would think he held dear—and buys a Harley. With leathers, beard, and a fresh tattoo, he roars off to see the world.

"Back in the Second Passage," Robert Hemfelt explains,

"the couple should have said good-bye to the grand illusion of childhood. That illusion promises that 'somewhere out there, there exists a perfect parent figure, someone who can give me all the answers and take care of me.' Saying good-bye to that illusion involves both abandoning the notion and grieving its loss. The myth of the perfect superparent is very, very, powerful."

The myth exists whether the biological parents are alive or dead. Ideally, it's been put to rest by now, if not in the Second Passage, at least in the Third. If the marriage partners have not yet said their emotional good-byes to the parents; if they have not yet grieved and abandoned the illusion of the perfect parent out there somewhere; it will erupt here in the Fourth Passage and erupt with a vengeance.

The external evidence of this eruption is a particularly virulent mid-life crisis. Men and women both will go to one of two extremes. Both extremes are sides of the same coin—the futile search for the perfect parent in disguise as the perfect mate. We call one side Disillusionment and the other side Overillusionment.

Disillusioned

Here is the person with the prototypical mid-life crazies you hear about. That man or woman is the cynical, embittered soul who deliberately turns away from his or her established foundations. It's the woman who divorces and settles in California to work in a health food store or weave hammocks. It's the businessman, a deacon in his church, who one day quits his job and moves to the Bahamas.

A woman we'll call Becky tells her story. "I grew up hearing that if I was the perfect mother and wife, if I found a satisfying career or hobby, I'd have the perfect good life. No difficult decisions, no hard choices. Perfect, perfect, perfect. Hah!

"My father taught himself computers when computers were just getting started. By the time they were big, he was in upper management and really knew how to use them.

He'd guessed right, you might say, and rode the crest of the wave right to the top. He sure seemed to me like he had all the answers, and he thought he did, too.

"Whatever Daddy said was true, even when I was twenty. I guess I was a late bloomer. I was out of college before I realized my father was just as fallible as everyone else. Incidentally, he's never yet figured that out. At least, he's never admitted it.

"I married a man who didn't make mistakes, either. George seemed to have all the answers. He took care of me; I didn't have to work. The prophecy of having a perfect life if you'll just be the perfect little mother seemed to be working. Then one day he accused our daughter Gretchen of stealing a twenty out of his wallet. She was eighteen at the time, just finishing school. I remember so clearly. She swore she didn't do it.

"I was siding with him automatically, like I always did, when I realized she couldn't have done it. She was with me at the grocery store, but her brother was alone in the house at the time. Greg was sixteen. So I told George, 'no, it has to be Greg,' and he turned on me. He claimed I was falsely accusing Greg because Gretchen was my pet, and then he just turned me off. Paid no attention to anything I said. He spanked her; I mean, really spanked her; eighteen years old! and told her to give the twenty back. She didn't have it, of course. So he confined her to her room.

"I was in shock for three days. I couldn't believe it. And then it hit me, in wave after wave. All the times he was wrong, or he could have been wrong, and I never paid attention. All the times he treated the kids unjustly and me unjustly, too.

"Gretchen left home the next day, and instantly he set up all these conditions she'd have to meet before he'd allow her to come back. A week later she married a real wretch of a kid. He said it was all her fault, of course.

"I hung in for a couple more years, then I left. It was so freeing, at first! I searched out all the things I'd been missing in my life. But finally, it ended up they were still missing. George has another wife now." She studies her hands wistfully. "And I have AIDS."

Becky's story is tragically common in several ways. For one thing, once disillusionment struck, Becky painted George black. No balanced view, no realistic appraisal. We happen to know George. He is not at all the ogre she describes. He certainly made mistakes, and had trouble admitting his mistakes, but he made many excellent choices as well. He had problems with control issues, serious problems, but he worked hard to understand and overcome them. Becky could not accept that he would change, or that he could have flaws and still meet her needs.

Typically also, all that she abandoned seemed hollow to her. For another, nothing she used to replace what she had abandoned offered any hope or meaning. That, too, is highly typical. You see, she was trying to find in all those things the surrogate perfect parents: pat answers, black and white choices, something or someone to save her from pain and wrong decisions.

Of course her mind told her no such perfection exists. But the heart rules. In Becky's heart, once the bubble burst, nothing at all was sacred anymore. By far the most tragic part: Becky has not been able to come back to the God who had been so precious to her at one time. She's lost trust in Him as well.

Overillusioned

The other side of the coin appears on the surface to be just the opposite of Becky's response. Actually, it rises from exactly the same cause and is equally potent. The overillusioned person latches on for dear life to some powerful authority figure or authority source. The overillusioned person will find someone or something to be believed in absolutely, to be trusted totally.

Garret Haynes went that way. A Fourth Passage husband and father, he suddenly and precipitously switched from his mainstream church to a small radical church, taking his family with him. Garret's wife Martha didn't understand. She missed the friendship and fellowship their church had provided for years. But he assured her the friendships and fellowship would be deeper in this new situation, so she went along with it.

In Garret's new church she found an extremely rigid pastor who seemed more than willing to tell each person in his flock how to live his or her life. She chafed under his stringent rules, but Garret embraced them eagerly. Martha disagreed with the pastor arbitrary habit of interpreting Scripture in strange ways and then claiming his interpretation was God's. She tried to talk to Garret about her doubts and misgivings, to no avail.

Sensing her rebellion, the pastor called upon Garret to straighten his wife out. Rather than serving as a spokesperson for God, the pastor seemed to want to "play god" in both their lives. The pastor objected not so much to her theology as to her dress and behavior, both perfectly normal for her prior church but against the rules in this one. She argued forcefully against salvation-through-works, again to no avail. When Garret and his pastor delivered the ultimatum—this church or an eternity in hell—she risked eternity by returning to her prior church. Fortunately, her true friends in Christ welcomed her back and supported her warmly.

Martha is in counseling with her pastor now, trying to come to terms with the fact that she has probably lost Garret to a cult-like group.

Like Garret, individuals and couples taking this other extreme, literally take it to the extreme. They hunger intensely for all the answers. And like Garret's new pastor, there is usually someone out there ready to trade absolute answers for absolute devotion.

Typically, the person going through disillusionment or overillusionment will do so in more than one dimension. That person is also extremely vulnerable to political manipulation or financial scams, for example. In counseling we find so many persons in this Fourth Passage who have dumped their life savings, and thereby their financial security, into questionable schemes that promise absolute results.

Seeking Answers

"What can I do?" Martha keeps asking. "I watch Garret sink deeper and deeper into this other group. I refuse to call them a church. They're certainly not associated with any denomination or other body of believers. I feel helpless."

In a way, Martha is indeed utterly helpless in terms of what she alone can do to alter the situation.

Were Garret's crisis fairly mild, she could approach him through loving confrontation. We recommend talking it through, husband and wife together, when either spouse notices that the other is slipping into a pattern that could be considered a crisis in the making.

The cure, so to speak, is to accept the fiction of the myth that one human or human institution has all the answers, and then grieve the loss. The myth must be put to rest. We recommend, too, that if this problem appears in the Fourth Passage that some clause be inserted in the revised marriage contract we will discuss in the last chapters.

But if Garret is completely over the rail, so to speak, loving confrontation will not reach him. Professional counseling sometimes does, but the person grasping at the dream of a perfect parent, however distorted that dream may be, often will not respond to conventional therapy. A wall of denial seals out reason. As in Garret's case, that person is probably clinging to an authority figure who rejects any threat to his or her control.

"If someone sees their spouse becoming that embittered or that overillusioned, they need outside help," Robert Hemfelt concludes. "If the illusion that an all-powerful parent is out there has been growing and festering, unresolved, throughout adult life, my spouse will probably be willing to jettison anything and everything. When the couple recognizes that serious distortion exists, in addition to counseling, they will want to add right into the contract some kind outside accountability. Enlist a trusted friend, counselor, or pastor."

And let us add this disclaimer: In no way are we casting the spiritual teaching of any church or denomination in a bad light. Garret's newfound church possessed no outside accountability and recognized no law save its own. Garret's new legalism was grinding his marriage up. Therein lies the red flag of warning.

The Last Good-bye

Myths have fled, parents have been recast as friends and mentors. There is one more good-bye you have to make and that is to your youth.

Chapter 5

Decisions the Loss of Your Youth Brings

"**Y**outh and vigor are great. Your twenties were great as you firmed up your commitments, laid out goals; you decided how your own family would run. The thirties are tremendously productive, high energy times.

"Then the forties. You can't see as well, your hair is thinning, your waist is flabbier no matter how much you work out. Then the fifties. Your parents are starting to die off, you yourself are slowing down physically . . . Mid-life is tough. In my opinion, maybe one of the hardest ages."

Whose opinion? Dr. Frank Minirth's. The man who gave talks on beating the odds—the farm boy who completed medical school, his residency, and seminary—suddenly found the odds taking a turn against him:

"I hit mid-life, one parent died, aunts and uncles died, my father-in-law died, my mortality became evident, a child got ill, my responsibilities increased. Mid-life is hard, *very* hard."

You, too, are wrestling with the odds at this stage of your life. Things are piling up all around you and you may be fighting an uphill battle to climb out from under them. You wake up one morning and the bones creak, the muscles are stiff and you didn't even work out the day before. You're getting old. Either it hits you all at once or a little bit at a time. But you are aging. To accomplish the third task of this

Fourth Passage: Grieve the Particular Losses; you also have to accept the loss of your youth.

Loss of Youth

Rob Millen strode out on the tennis court with his partner, Bill Peters, ready to shine in their company's tournament. Hey, they were good and they knew it. The draw matched them against two flabby young nerds from the computer department. They spun for serve.

"Have you seen these guys play?" Bill asked nervously as he walked back to the baseline. "They can't be more than twenty-five."

"True, but we'll get them on the ol' lob." Rob grinned. "Remember; old age and perfidy always wins over youth and honesty."

Zing! The ball came whizzing past. Rob swung and missed.

"Was that in?" the young buck asked.

"Did you even see it?" Rob hissed at Bill.

The server's partner at the net said, "Looked in to me. Great serve—an ace!"

Over the next two painful hours, Rob and Bill were so thoroughly trounced by the younger team they felt fortunate to play the consolation round.

Little changes wrought by the steady march of birthdays turn out to be not so little.

One of the little things that hits squarely now is a change in health and vigor. For women it's called menopause although other aging processes like osteoporosis add to it. For men, there's also a menopause of sorts. We discussed the sexual changes in Chapter Three. Let's focus now on the physical changes that accompany mid-life and aging.

Rob's wife got just as big a dose of reality as he did, though not on the tennis court.

Goodbye, Lost Health

Annie Warden Millen, having married off her last nestling Beth Anne, felt at loose ends, as if someone had let all the air out of her tires. Like a stalk of wilted celery. She got a medical examination with all the extras, right down to a fecal smear. She got her Pap test and mammogram. There had to be something wrong physically for her to feel this shot down all the time.

Everyone knows that progressive physical deterioration may begin to show itself more dramatically around fifty, but no one who has not yet reached that age dares ask just how much.

Apart from all the diseases and disabilities associated with aging (not all of which actually are a function of aging), there's menopause. Women with low self-esteem, women already uncertain of themselves, dread this clear, bold evidence that they're getting old. A few hearty souls, so relieved that the inconvenience and mess are finally done, send out announcements. The attitudes of most women fall somewhere in between. These days, medicine can make subtle adjustments to ease the problems traditionally associated with menopause, from mood swings to osteoporosis.

Indeed, medicine now offers a growing arsenal of tools to deal with the diseases and disabilities of aging. Replacement hips, hearing aids and such can do much toward alleviating problems. We still have our troubles; but it's easier than it used to be.

We counsel every reader regardless of his or her age to stay on top of potential health problems. Keep a lid on them. Many can be minimized or solved if caught in time. We now have the ability to live longer and more productively. Tap into it.

It is appropriate—in fact, it's essential—that you work through the reality of your fading physical vitality. Working through your changing health involves, paradoxically, both accepting the changes, and vigorously, yet appropriately, combating the changes. You need not succumb to it and give up. You should not. But neither can you glibly deny what is happening.

"Your ticker's fine," Annie's doctor announced, "but your female system is going to need attention one of these days. Your frequent and irregular periods are one reason you don't feel very great. You're not anemic, technically, but it's pulling your blood count down."

"What do we do about it?"

"Nothing for now. Come back and see me again in six months or a year."

Annie left his office fuming. Easy for a male to say. He didn't have to live with this constant lack of pep, or the messy inconvenience of irregular periods. More than that was bothering her, though. If she had a broken leg, they'd fix it. If she caught pneumonia, they'd medicate it. But her problems were so vague, her symptoms so diffuse, there was no clear answer, no easy fix. That's the trouble with the results of aging, Annie bemoaned. They're so indefinite.

If you are entering this Fourth Passage of marriage, or have reached that age, you are beginning, like Annie, to feel the effects of all those years of wear and tear on your body. Such losses are properly grieved through, as are any others.

Let us go through the grief process again, from a somewhat different angle. We emphasize it because it is so centrally important to your negotiation of all the passages of marriage.

First, we invite you to list some physical differences, both positive and negative, between your body today and what it was twenty years ago. This could be what the kids call an organ recital—"my leg hurts, my liver's bum, my . . . ." Was there a weight change?

1. _____
2. _____
3. _____
4. _____
5. _____

Now list some differences of performance. What is your body less capable of doing now (we've already dealt with sexual performance and abilities in Chapter Three. This portion is non-sexual)? Is it better at some things than when you were young?

1. _____
2. _____
3. _____
4. _____
5. _____

Any serious diseases or accidents you've come through?

1. _____
2. _____
3. _____

Those items that improved over the years are worthy of celebration.

"When I married my Bob," a friend confides, "he was six feet four and weighed a hundred and fifty-five pounds. A finishing nail casts a wider shadow. I don't know what I saw in him. He looked terrible. Now, thirty-two years later, he's picked up about thirty pounds, and he's a hunk. Beefier shoulders and arms, especially. Celebrate? Honey, you bet! But it took a lot of southern cooking to get him up there."

List three things that improved over the years:

1. _____
2. _____
3. _____

Celebrate! We always encourage patients and friends to celebrate both things that are good, and things that could be worse than they are.

Now go through the items of loss one by one. Have you adequately grieved the loss of youthful health? If no such feelings come to mind, perhaps your grieving is not complete. Thinking back, can you remember feelings of shock and denial about those items of loss you listed? Write a few brief words to remind yourself of how you felt.

How about anger? Perhaps it was brief; perhaps it hung about your head like a cloud for years. Tell about it.

Depression. Anger turned inward. It may come on you simply as "a bad case of the blahs." Has depression been a part of your response to the ravages of aging?

In what ways have you been bargaining with the aging process, stopping it in its tracks so to speak? Wrinkle cream? Hair color? Cosmetic surgery? Medications and vitamins? Be honest. And what has it benefitted you?

Great sadness accrues. Can you describe an occasion or occasions when this phase of grief loomed large in your life as the truth of aging forced itself upon you?

After the emotions are cleansed comes resolution, and acceptance. The process of physical aging has been programmed into you along with all your other genetic attributes. Every human being ages so similarly that we can often guess a person's chronological age within a few years. In short, God designed for you to grow old. In this fallen world every blessing is sullied, but it is a blessing no less. To accept that God knows what He's doing—yes, even when He came up with this aging business—provides a wonderful freedom from anxiety and despair.

That is the attitude of the six of us as we come to terms with God's inevitable process. What is yours? Can you

phrase it in a few sentences? Let your mind roll; let your true
feelings emerge.

_____

_____

_____

_____

    What prevents our resolution and acceptance of the griev-
ing process? Many hurdles exist, and the world around us
doesn't help.

Resolution Blockers

    Nearly every ad, television program, magazine, movie,
and newspaper carries some message that aging isn't good,
and that it should be fought every step of the way.

    It's a common joke that women lie about their age. No
wonder, when society stresses youth as opposed to aging.
Programmed into women from an early age is the innuendo
that old women are unattractive crones. Women spend enormous amounts of time and energy trying to look and stay
young. Hanging over women's heads looms the Sword of
Damocles: Seize youth, or risk the loss of your mate to a
younger, more attractive woman.

    In the business world, too, age is seen as more of a handi-
cap than a benefit. Men or women reaching their fifties are
seen as short-timers—to be put out to pasture until they
reach retirement age or, if possible, dumped before the company has to pay retirement benefits. It is falsely assumed that
productivity significantly declines with age. As a result, the
business world is losing an enormous source of experience.

    So how does one survive the crises of middle age against
these immense odds? There's little support from society and
our culture which worships youth and wants to hide from
age. Fortunately, as the population pyramid changes with
the baby boom generation approaching middle age, more
and more support will come for aging—it's a matter of de-
mographics.

Probably the most crucial test, though, comes from you as an individual making the right decisions when faced with the crises of aging during this Fourth Passage.

Decision Time

Pretend you are a college student taking a course in entomology. You and your coursemates have been out in the field scooping up every insect you can find, because you have to present a collection of at least one hundred families by the end of the term. You now have killing jars with a plethora of weird bugs you've never seen before. For this you're paying good tuition money?

With long tweezers you reach in at random and bring out a beetle. Peachy. There are nearly 29,000 kinds of beetles just in North America. Ah well. You know the order is Coleoptera without having to look it up. That's the easy part. You turn to a dichotomous key.

Key to the principal families of Coleoptera.
(1A) Is the head drawn out into a slender beak (go to 2) or
(1B) is it not? (go to 17)

It's not. You find key feature 17.
(17A) Does the coxa of the hind leg divide the first abdominal segment (go to 18)
(17B) or does it not? (go to 36)

You put your beetle on its back under the dissecting scope and peer. It does. You go to 18.

Eventually, by choosing between the A and B options of the sets of key characters, yes or no, you learn that your beetle is a Carabid, a ground beetle of the genus *Calosoma*. It's an agile hunter that climbs shrubs and small trees in search of caterpillars. It usually hides by day, and indeed you found it under dry leaves. Your faceless science specimen has taken on a personality and become interesting.

Decision time. Biology students detest dichotomous keys even as they utterly depend upon them, in part because most people hate to make decisions. If you go wrong on one little decision at the front of the key, you've lost your chance at identification. You go bounding down some false bunny trail that leads to the wrong final choice or, more frequently, no choice at all.

You're going to have to make a raft of decisions in this stage of life, just as does the entomology student with a key in hand.

Debi Newman points out, "You can't be asking questions about mid-life now, and reevaluating. The time for questions is done. You're there. This is now the time of either crisis or growth, a major Y in the tree of decisions. Crisis will either destroy you or generate new intimacy and growth."

A dichotomous key works because you rule out one thing at a time. It's not a bad way to approach other decisions as well. For Annie Millen, her first decision was to get a full-blown physical. She knew something must be wrong with her physically for her to feel so run down and blah. That's actually a very healthy decision. Rule out any physical ailments first. Get them treated. In Annie's case, though, the physical came up with no concrete answers. Now she had to try another decision, the next key character, finding out what's missing, what would fill her void. She would find that one solution was her marriage. When she started working on her marriage, her well-being improved. That's just how effective this Passage can be to a person. Frequently, that's not the case, though. People tend to think that it's the marriage that's the problem. They want out, while there's still time to find another relationship with someone else.

Life's Dichotomous Key

In counseling we often see major changes in persons who find their youth slipping away.

The first bilateral decision every married person in this age group must make is:

1.   A. Do I bloom where I'm planted, so to speak, and go with the flow? (go to 2)

B. Do I undertake what the psychologists call a geographic cure?

The aging marital partner who chooses B then has four major choices that we encounter constantly in people vainly seeking their youth. They obtain a divorce, have an affair to prove they've still got it, make a radical job change, or take "geographical change" literally and move somewhere.

Understand, there is nothing wrong with making changes at mid-life, a course correction, if you will, provided it's healthy change. The Fourth Passage couple has new options and new freedoms. This may well be the time to sell the house and undertake the missions project you've always talked about, or whatever. Blind change to compensate for loss is not healthy.

Change of Job or Residence

How do you know if this change is healthy or not? Are you trying to negate the losses or actually taking good advantage of the opportunities this stage of life offers? You can pretty much tell the difference by assuming that you have chosen A: That you can bloom where you are planted.

"If I am working with persons in this stage of life," says Robert Hemfelt, and they're contemplating a change of career or residence, I make this point: If the change is healthy, it will be just as valid six or twelve months from now as it is this moment. I will counsel, 'Allow it to incubate.' If it doesn't dim with time, then make the move."

And always attend any decision of that sort with much, much prayer.

An aspect of blooming where one is planted might be to go back to the job that seems so stagnant and try to make positive changes. The very fact of thinking positively, and trying to act positively, puts you in a better mental position to make good decisions.

Lousy decisions, even if they seem wonderful at the moment, will tend to pass in half a year or so.

2.   A. I'm going to be aware of the fact I can go overboard now, and struggle to keep an even keel. (on to 3)

   B. I'll go to extreme with either disillusionment or over-illusionment.

You read about disillusionment and overillusionment and the havoc they can wreak at this stage of life. They can be triggered by losses of youth as much as anything else. Be aware of them, and make response A your goal.

3.   A. I will own my projections (go on to good health in emotions and relationships).

   B. I did not own my projections in the past and I will not now (suffer one of three consequences).

Own? Projections? These are common psychological terms for two important mental phenomena. To own is to recognize and accept a reality of some sort. When you're angry, for example, you either own your anger and discharge it appropriately, or refuse to admit you're angry and bury it somehow. Nothing buried ever just goes away. It seethes. It festers. It erupts.

To project is to take some trait of your own and stick it on someone else. "Projection" is an apt term; think of it as taking a trait such as anger and projecting it like a movie onto another person, the screen. Obviously, since married couples are in such close proximity, they often use each other as the screen.

What gets projected? In our culture, at least until recently, men were not supposed to express tenderness, sensitivity, compassion, and sometimes even sensuality. Macho sex was raw and to the point—a drum roll, not a violin duet. This age group feels that proscription acutely. It's what we grew up with. Since men are not supposed to feel that, the wife ends up carrying all the couple's tenderness.

So what can go wrong? It seems like a convenient arrange-ment. The problem is that men do indeed have a tender side. They do respond with compassion and sensitivity. When what he has been projecting comes home, the man at this stage might come home one day announcing his desire to move into a commune, play guitar, and write poetry. He might enter into a mid-life affair, unconsciously believing that since his wife thusfar has been the carrier of his projected tenderness, here is where his flair for romance will come gushing out.

Almost universally, women project their power, anger, and aggression, onto the male. These are perceived as male attributes by the culture we grew up in. The perfect lady, she has to this point let her husband carry all the aggression and anger in the union. But that cannot last.

Typically, once the kids leave home and her interests broaden or awaken, the lady discovers that she's more than she had guessed. Again, in a typical case, the wife who re-enters the work force discovers that she's indeed talented and able to make a go of it. She may get drunk on power, in a sense, because to this time she's given over all power to her husband. She may become ferociously angry at her husband for keeping her out of the job market. Probably, he wasn't, really. In reality she was making that choice herself.

None of this is rational. Projection is never rational. And there is certainly nothing wrong with a career. The problem is the difficulties failure to own projections cause.

Projections can be positive or negative. The man who projects onto his wife his tenderness is projecting a very positive attribute. But it's projection all the same and therefore dangerous. The man or woman who projects anger, a negative trait, onto the spouse is no better off.

Usually, married couples have been coming to terms with their projections steadily over the years. The way of thinking might go something like this: "I've been angry with Fred for years because of his constant procrastination, but I see myself procrastinating just as badly." "I wish my wife were not so wrapped up in her job, but I spend just as many hours in overtime." The constantly calm, quiet wife who at first projected all her anger and frustrations onto her husband, starts to blow up occasionally herself. She is starting to own her anger.

When married couples do not over the years come to recognize the traits they've been dumping off on others, here is
where all the unhealthy projections explode at once. They
will explode in any of three ways:

1) The marital partner will intensify the projection. Here
is polarization in new dress. The woman who hardly ever got
angry before never ever does now. The problem is, of
course, her husband becomes angrier and angrier. And he
doesn't really see why, and that makes him angrier still. The
man who rarely evinced tenderness in the past doesn't
bother at all anymore. The wife hungers more and more for
gentle love, and finds none. Negative projections often end
up handled this way.

2) The marital partner will reject or destroy the screen.
Divorce is the common method of destruction.

"I don't know," was May's constant response when
someone asked her why she was divorcing Al. It was the
truth. She had no idea, except that she couldn't stand Al
anymore. So she put forth all the standard reasons: We're
incompatible; we've grown apart; we have no common
ground anymore. She missed the biggie: Al had always been
the screen of her projected aggressiveness. She despised aggressiveness and refused to own any at all. It was either come
to terms with her aggressiveness or get rid of it permanently.

3) The marital partner will replace the trait, whatever it is,
with actual anger, and project the anger onto the screen.
Need we say, this way out is bound to make the screen's life
a living nightmare.

Dr. Hemfelt explains. "Say I'm a woman who for thirty
years has been projecting all my authority, power, and
strength onto you, my husband. Suddenly late in mid-life,
my youth is leaving. My world is changing. I turn on you,
husband, my projection screen, and become intensely, viv-
idly angry with you. I blame you for sapping my strength,
and I am furious."

A double image is being projected upon itself here. The

amazing anger is being dumped upon the husband, but he's also carrying the power yet—feelings on top of feelings.

An example is a husband who for thirty-two years always projected onto his wife the ability to reach out to people. He had no friends of his own and no social life. In reality, he, like every other human being, needed his own social life, his own circle of friends.

He became involved in a consuming affair with an outgoing woman, surprisingly, four years older than he. He and his wife discussed separation and divorce. He blamed her, and her alone. "You dominated me," he fumed, livid. "You took all the friends. Everyone who knows about us takes your side. They can't see how controlling you are. How you have them bamboozled!" In reality he is coming to terms with his need for the friends he does not have. And he's turning all his anger about his felt need onto the woman who carried his social burden for him for three decades.

Supposing now that you have chosen 3A and have decided to own the projections you've fostered all these years. These projections are similar to the hidden contracts we've talked about, but they tend to be more specific.

What are your spouse's traits, good and bad? List off a bunch.

Study the list. Which of those traits do you yourself absolutely lack?

If you were you talking about this to a friend, and it was the friend who lacked those traits, would you consider it normal? If you have to say, "Well, it's not normal for most people, but it is for me," there may be a problem.

Keep in mind that good health requires that you bring these to the surface so you can come to terms with them. Grieve the losses just as you have been, and from now on seek opportunities to take better responsibility for the traits common to all men and women. Besides messing up your relationships, these projections have been killing your dreams.

Ways to Cope with Aging

Not all dreams have died. By now you may be living many of your dreams—if not exactly, at least close. This is the passage also where lovers can really start growing. This is where they either renew love or live in the pits. Too often, usually for lack of the effort to change, couples live in the pits unless something jolts them into revitalizing their love.

The challenge sounds simple:

Bond together as a couple into deeper unity and love.

But it's not so simple. Empty nest, stagnation, disappointment, even, sometimes, early retirement ("Twice as much husband; half as much money") work against unity. So does plain old inertia—a lack of impetus to make changes.

Working with you to complete the challenge are memories and history. You've made it this far, despite some ridiculous escapades. The end is worth shooting for! Perhaps it's even worth shooting for with gusto.

Chapter 6

New Relationships with Your Children

*A*sk Annie thirteen years ago if she would dread an empty nest that morning she walked into her kitchen. Beth Anne, then age seven, perched on a chair at the stove, making breakfast. Pancakes, bowls, spoons, and flour were everywhere. Broken egg on the floor. The dog licking something up over by the fridge. The stove burners still smoking where batter globs had burnt. The mixer beaters, perched on the edge of the counter, dripping batter into the open utensil drawer. "Goodbye to children? I'll pack this minute."

Frustrations aside, there comes a day when the fledglings leave the nest. Couples whose nestlings are still home assume that saying goodbye means packing the stuffed toys in the attic, handing the kid his suitcase and waving him off at the front door. There is much more to it than that.

The Period of Renewal and Death of a Relationship—

The Empty Nest

We spoke of saying good-bye to your parents in the last chapter. By now you're probably thinking: "I've done quite enough grieving, thank you. And quite enough thinking about the losses of my life. Why do you keep harping on them?"

Because life is tough, as the old saying goes. Life is full of losses. And we can't say the following enough: Without successfully grieving and coming to terms with these losses, you will get stuck in a passage. You must resolve the losses that are inevitable within your life to successfully complete one passage and go to the next. Without grieving these losses, you will get stuck on base and walk away scoreless at the end of the inning.

If your children have already left your home residentially, have they emotionally and financially also? If they have not left, how well prepared are you for their exodus?

How About You?

What do you savor about the prospect of the children leaving home (whether it has occurred yet or not) and what do (did) you dread? List each thought separately. Celebrate the ones you savor about the leaving—"Freedom, pure freedom. I can cook dinner when and if I please. I can't wait."

So now list those items you can hardly wait for when the children finally leave:

1. _____
2. _____
3. _____
4. _____

Grieve those you dread: "What am I going to do with all the free time? I'll be so lonely. My main occupation is about to end." Annie Warden Millen had some real grieving to do after Beth Anne's wedding. Her loneliness was a very real loss, not unlike a feeling of abandonment. If she was to successfully pass through this stage of parenting and find a renewed relationship with her fledgling, she had to successfully grieve this loss.

Now list those items you dread when your nest is vacated:

1. _____
2. _____

3. _____

4. _____

How did your parents handle the empty nest thing? Look first at surface indications (which may all appear just fine).

At what ages did you and your siblings leave home residentially? _____

financially? _____

List a couple things your parents said or did (overt indications) as the first child left:

_____

_____

What did they say and do when the last one left?

_____

_____

How many rooms formerly used by the children were converted to new uses and how many have been kept the same ("Still little Bobby's room" when Bobby left home five years ago)? _____

Now look for sub-surface attitudes.

What indications, perhaps more felt than seen, tell you your parents made peace with their children's departure (some examples: they converted your sister's room into a sewing room; they moved the dining room furniture around to better serve a close couple than to feed a mob)?

_____

_____

What can you think of that might tell you your parents never quite came to grips with their children's departure (perhaps they left all your brother's sports posters up on his wall, or they refuse to change anything in the house, just in case someone should come back home)?

_____

_____

The patterns your parents set will probably determine the personal attitude your conscious mind doesn't even know about.

Based on what you've just looked at, list several good

things and several not-so-good things you see in your parents' attitude toward the empty nest. Which ones do you consider exemplary?

1. _____
2. _____
3. _____
4. _____

Which ones do you think you ought to avoid?

1. _____
2. _____
3. _____
4. _____

How do these lists compare with your own lists at the beginning of this chapter? We often find that they are similar.

Assuming your children have not yet left home, what specific steps do you intend to take to avoid your parents' mistakes or rough spots?

1. _____
2. _____
3. _____
4. _____

If your children have left, what would you do differently if you had it to do again?

_____
_____

Should you discuss what you've discovered here with your adult children? Perhaps the insight you've made here will release them from the unfinished business you placed upon them.

Cut the Financial Cord

A large element of goodbye is letting the kids go financially and emotionally as well as residentially. This is a sticky wicket because no two cases are the same.

Robert Hemfelt relates, "Take the example of a man who has a perpetual student at home. The daughter is twenty-four. The man's problem is his wife. She wants the girl to remain in their home while she finishes her schooling, and Dad wants the kid out.

"This man has to deal with Mom, and somehow convince her it's best for the daughter to become responsible for herself. If the girl had only a semester or two to go, perhaps they could let it slide. But she switches majors, takes light class loads—the end is nowhere in sight.

"It is most important that neither parent act behind the other's back. Undercutting each other will lead to disaster when this couple finally are alone."

How would a counselor help in this situation? First they would look for underlying meanings to the parents actions —hidden agendas and emotional incest for two examples. Neither of these were at work in this instance. Thus, on the practical level, this man might negotiate a deal with his daughter. Let her live there, but pay market value rent. Get behind in the rent and out you go.

In negotiations, the parents must also both agree to whatever the deal might be. If one parent sees it differently (and the mother certainly did) that person must not just keep quiet and resent the whole thing. Any negotiation must be mutually acceptable all across the board.

When Robert Hemfelt last heard, this man's daughter had found a cheaper rent arrangement and was living near the university in a five-bedroom house with four other girls.

Lacking a counselor, how should a couple approach a financial issue with their departed or not yet departed children? As we mentioned, hidden agenda searches come first. Your attitude towards your children's financial independence will be affected in some way by your parents' attitudes.

For example, take a client of ours, Brad Jameson—the owner of a successful plumbing supply company. He had worked hard, scraping and fighting for what he had. Now, he and his wife live in a very exclusive section of Denver. They were financially set as they approached retirement.

"I had no help from Pop." He bragged to us one day. "My kids have it easy compared to what I had."

"So everything you have now, you've earned. Correct?" we asked.

"You bet. I worked from the bottom, went to school at nights while working as a plumber's apprentice. I know what hard times are."

"Now that you've made it, what are you going to do with all your wealth?"

"Charities, the church. But mostly I'm going to enjoy it —Marge and me both. We're going to have fun. You know the bumper sticker that says: 'We're spending our kids' inheritance.' That's us."

"There's nothing wrong with that. We're glad you're looking forward to retirement. But Marge has told us that you have a problem with the kids."

"It's Jeff and his new wife. They want to borrow some money for a downpayment on a house. I say let them earn the downpayment like I did and then buy the house when they can. They can rent in the meantime."

"Have they come to you for money before?"

"No, although I did put Jeff through school. I wanted him to take over the business. But noooo, he had to become a veterinarian. Not only is he making much less money, he had to go to school four more years. He's got himself so much in debt with his new practice that he can't get a loan for the house without a substantial downpayment."

Brad's position on this issue, on the surface, may seem reasonable. Until we dug deep within his psyche and found the real reasons: a time-release capsule based on his family-of-origin.

When we explored Brad's family history, we found, indeed, he grew up in poverty. His father died an untimely death when Brad was still in high school. Brad had to drop out of school to help support the family. He planned to go to school and even had visions of college once all his brothers and sisters were out of the house and Mom was able to support herself.

But things didn't exactly go according to Brad's plan. Brad's youngest brother, Davey, wouldn't leave. He finished high school, barely, and then stayed home with Mom—working at this and that part-time job. Suddenly Brad had to support his mom and Davey for what seemed like the rest of his life. This situation finally blew up and Brad wasn't on speaking terms with his mother for a period. Eventually, Brad was able to reduce his support of his mom and younger brother. But he never got the chance to finish high school or go on to college. By the time he could, he was immersed in his own business and supporting his own growing family.

This childhood deeply instilled a time-release capsule that popped when Brad's own children left home. Because he himself had to do it on his own, he felt deep down that his children also had to. Fearing getting sucked dry, he wouldn't lend them any money no matter how reasonable the request. And, worse yet, his unwavering position had created intense unspoken conflict between him and his wife, which is what landed them in our counsel.

"After all," his wife, Marge told us, "it's not like we're hurting. We have more than enough. And, Brad, being the financial wizard he is, has us all set for retirement. We can afford to indulge the kids a bit. He didn't seem to mind when they were home. It's just been since they left. It's like he's afraid they'll turn out like his brother."

Marge was onto something with that last comment. Brad was so intensely afraid that his children would take advantage of him like his brother did of his mom, that he not only cut the apron strings, he downright cauterized them.

Another aspect which works against coming to terms with the loss of your children is emotional incest. A counselor will look for this phenomenon when a couple is having trouble with an empty nest. So many times a child can become a surrogate spouse. It's particularly common with broken marriages. Also, when a couple drift apart, one or both may attach to a child for emotional support. But how would a parent see that? We suggest asking yourself these true-or-false questions to help identify the problem if it exists:

_____ If my spouse and my child are available during my free time, I'd rather be with my child.

_____ My child and I seem to have more in common than my spouse and I do.

_____ My child understands better than my spouse does when I talk about my problems, whether the child is a factor in the problem or not.

_____ My spouse is unavailable when I most need to talk.

Now think about your answers. If the criterion for the strength of a bond were the amount of time spent with a family member (other than a small child, of course, who requires constant monitoring), with whom would you be bonded most firmly?

If the criterion be the amount of time thinking and worrying about a person, with whom are you most strongly bonded?

If the criterion be the most emotional response you make —being angry with, being proud of, being comfortable with —who wins?

If each family member is in a separate room, which room are you likely to find yourself in?

Should your child come out ahead of your spouse in more than one of these instances, or if you answer "true" to the above questions more than once, start giving a cold, hard eye to your relationship with your child (if you have children, usually one stands out; emotional incest rarely happens between a parent and more than one child at a time).

Whatever decisions are made about weaning children away financially, they must be mutually arranged by the parents. Any other situation invites friction and resentment.

Joan, Annie's friend, and her husband, Harold, were able to use the strength of their marriage to do just this. Their son Tom was on his second marriage, something they hadn't approved of in the first place. Anxious to get out of his first marriage, he had quickly negotiated a bad child support provision. Now he was supporting two families on his meager salary. His second wife didn't work outside of the home, so they were constantly asking his parents for money. Joan and Harold were getting a little tired of always having to bail their son out of his financial crises.

Joan hung up the phone one evening, "Tom wants another loan," she told Harold.

Harold took off his reading glasses and looked up at her from the evening paper. "What else is new? He hasn't paid any on the other ones."

"It's for a good reason," Joan said.

"It's always for a good reason," Harold answered. He sighed and put down the paper. "We've got to put a stop to this, our bucket is only so full."

"I know, but how?"

"Let's look at the options," Harold began. He pulled out a tablet of paper.

The two of them approached this problem as a team and brainstormed ideas. Not only did this help weather future crises, it provided creative solutions and, even better, further solidified their relationship.

Their solution to the above problem was to work with their attorney and draw up a proper loan agreement, consolidating all the past loans along with this new one. Their son was put on a payment plan with automatic payments taken directly from his salary. It sounds a bit harsh, but Joan and Harold had to have some sort of security that they would be repaid. Their retirement income was at stake.

Does this all mean we don't suggest helping out your children financially long after they've left the nest? Not at all. No, there can be appropriate ways to extend financial help. Usually you're in a better financial position than your children who are just starting out with new families. Just be careful of it becoming a habit and be careful of dependency

and resentment building up on either side (you and your
spouse) or your children. Remember, money is a powerful
symbol for nurturance and authority in a family system, and
money can be misused to sustain an inappropriate financial
umbilical cord across the generations. So each decision to
help your children must be made on a case-by-case basis,
with the benefits and disadvantages weighed not just for the
principals, but for all the extended family.

Another area that starts to pop when your children leave
home is any unrealized dreams you had for them as they
were growing up. These unfulfilled dreams need to be
grieved and resolved also.

Reconcile the Dreams

"Guilt," said a client we'll call Ralph. "I started out with
a thousand-dollar debt to the vocational school I attended,
and ended up with the best transmission place in town, with
three locations. We get more business than the big franchise
shops with their fancy advertising. But I lost my family in the
process."

Yes, that would generate some guilt. Ralph's priorities
cost him his first wife and their two children. "My girl, Gina.
She's so bright. Straight A's in school. . . . until she got
into drugs and dropped out. And my son. He's in the Army.
The Army. An NCO with no ambition to move further in
his military career." Ralph wagged his head.

Guilt.

By their Fourth Passage, many, many fathers feel as Ralph
felt, guilty for neglecting their marriage, and especially the
kids, in their drive to succeed. Their careers became a powerful part of their lives and their family, feeling unwanted
and neglected, wanders off. The marriage collapses.

Children do not always meet or exceed the parents' hopes
for them. They just don't turn out the way you intended.
Ralph's certainly didn't. And guilt is a natural response. So is
bitter disappointment. All that must be grieved.

Another client of ours, Charles, came face to face with

unrealized dreams with his son. "I had visions for my son: He'd excel in sports and school. Go to college on a football scholarship and become a doctor.

"A bit high, I admit. But I thought at least, he'd play ball and go to college. Matthew turned out quite different. He was small and uncoordinated. It seemed nothing that kid could do was right on the field. In midget football, his coach had the audacity to tell me that Matthew's heart wasn't in football. He was just playing because I wanted him to. He said Matthew would get hurt if we didn't get him off the team.

"A failure. My kid was a failure. His teen years were no better. Nothing Matthew tried was a success."

"Nothing?" we asked. "There must have been something your son was good at. Think hard."

"Well, the computer I guess. Matthew could play on it for hours. Could figure out the most intricate solution to a computer game."

"What's he doing now as an adult?" we asked.

"He ended up going to a vocational school in computer repair. No football scholarship and no doctor either."

"Is he happy?"

"Seems to be. Married a real nice girl. They live in a modest home near the airport. Not my idea of a good neighborhood, but they like it."

"And you're not happy?"

"Well, I guess it's this middle age stuff you read about. But I can't help but think I've been a failure. I haven't left any legacy behind on this earth to contribute something of value to society. Where did I go wrong with Matthew?"

It took lots and lots of talking and introspection to get Charles to see that he was unhappy because his son had not met his dream for him—his plans. Probably the hardest reality to accept with your children is that they will follow their own drummer, march to their own beat. After the years of parental guidance, adult children will more or less do what

they want to do in their lives. That's how it should be—
that's a healthy way for your children to turn out.

It is now, during this Fourth Passage, and when the nest is
emptied, that most people come face to face with this realization: My children didn't turn out like I thought they
would.

It's an unmet dream to be grieved. The children themselves, however, are a cause for rejoicing.

If your children have been into drugs, alcohol, criminal
behavior, or something else equally as serious, it's particularly hard to grieve this loss. But it must be done. The bottom line is that you are not ultimately responsible for your
children's destiny. You housebreak them and show them
right from wrong. You role model for them your own faith,
and beyond that, how they choose to accept or ignore God's
guidance is up to them, not you.

Coming to terms with the fact that your children are their
own decision-makers is one of the biggest steps you will
make as a parent. You saw them into the world. Now you
see them in it.

When you launch them from the nest, they'll fly—perhaps
not the way you think they should, but they'll fly.

Equally as dangerous are those cases where the children
indeed meet or exceed the parents' hopes. Then the parents
have to be as careful. It's easy to blot up a vicarious identity
with the successful children, putting your own identity and
your identity as a marital partner at risk. They are young,
they're making it big, and they're yours. With no trouble at
all you might cease to recognize that they are another generation, their own person, a different family now.

What About You?

Take a moment to think of the dreams you had for your
children. List them below. Do a separate list for each child.
Name: _____

    My dreams for him/her:

1. _____

2. _____

3. _____

4. _____

5. _____

Review your list for each child. Rejoice in those dreams which have been fulfilled or surpassed. What? They didn't meet *your* expectations? Very well, try making out the list over again with your *children's* dreams as you know them. Now how well are they fulfilled?

Examine your children's dreams and yours which were largely unmet. Resolve each unmet dream separately using the grieving process.

Incidentally, Ralph the transmission man actually has three children; the adult children of his first union and a four-year-old by his second wife. This time, he's stopping to smell the roses.

Death of One Relationship, Birth of Another

With the leaving of your children comes the opportunity for increased intimacy with them on a totally new level. No longer do you have the responsibility as the nurturing parent, although you can still be an advisor with all your experience. You and your spouse have the opportunity to build a new friendship with your children. As adults, you are now peers. More than any other childhood period, you can actually foster a friendship with your children. And don't forget their spouses or friends. You can now have access to these extended friendships through your children.

A healthy friendship with your child, in which the parent is no longer the primary authority figure, is not the same as the earlier child-parent relationship. Delightful and rewarding as this new friendship might be, the past must be grieved and put behind. Celebrate the new relationship; grieve the old one.

Another new relationship that can be celebrated at this stage of life is that with your friends. No longer restricted by childrearing, your friends and you can enjoy a greater freedom to socialize.

Chapter 7

New Relationships with Your Friends

"W ho wants to be responsible for dinner on Friday?" Joan's husband Harold asked the small gathering around their kitchen table. Annie and Rob were among the four couples at the table.

"We'll do dinner." Annie answered.

"Great. That takes care of meals. Now for entertainment. What do we want to do? Hike, just laze around, what?"

"I want to relax and sightsee. Just relax, no phones, no cars, no television, nothing but sun and water," one of the women answered.

"I'd like to hike up some of the side canyons. And see Rainbow Bridge." Joan added.

"I'd like to try my hand at waterskiing. It's been years. I hope I can still get up on skis." Rob Millen injected.

"That'll take care of more than one form of entertainment—comic relief." Harold chuckled.

"Very funny, Harold." Rob answered, but he smiled anyway.

These four couples had rented a houseboat together for a week at Lake Powell, Utah. They were in the midst of planning an eagerly-anticipated vacation together, just the eight of them.

Enhanced Friendships

By the time you've reached your Fourth Passage of marriage, you and your spouse have managed to foster a number of friendships with others, of varying degree, some as women friends, and some as male friends. We hope you have fostered a good many couple friendships, as well. It is exactly during this stage that you finally have some time and energy to give to those friendships. It is also at this time that you need the support which other adults in your age group can give you.

A church executive who found himself in a mid-life extramarital affair and was later restored to his wife said this about friendships: "I would encourage every man to have another man he can look eyeball to eyeball with and talk about tough issues of life; to be accountable to. Every man needs that kind of a friend." So does every woman. So does every couple.

Rob Millen benefitted from the advice of his friend Bill Peters as the two of them watched Kerri walk out of church one day.

"Very nice, huh?" Bill said. Kerri's athletic legs danced lightly along the sidewalk. She glowed with optimism and youth. "Strictly hands off, of course."

"Makes you think, though." Rob watched her disappear around the side of the building. He happened to know she usually parked her little Toyota in the far lot.

"Better watch it Rob, my boy. That's not just buying into trouble, that's taking out a loan."

"Why do I always have to look out for trouble? Suppose I want to live a little, take a chance."

Bill shot Rob a sharp glance. "Before you decide to live a little, do me a favor."

"What?"

"Call me up and we'll go for a cup of coffee."

Rob looked in his friend's eyes. He saw caring there, and

empathy. "Sure, maybe that's what I need after all. Someone to talk to. Annie's just . . . well, you know."

"Yes I do. I know exactly how it can be." Bill was Rob's age. His voice carried an authority no younger man could command.

The crises of middle age aren't just coming at you now. They're charging at you. They seem stronger, more intense. There's an urgency you didn't feel before to do, to experience, to reach. There is even an urgency in the losses that normally mark this passage of your marriage and your life— the loss of your youth, your parents, your children, some of your dreams. You hear the thunder of hoofbeats coming, and it sounds like hollow old age.

Old age is not hollow. But that's beside the point, a matter to consider later. Right now, the plus factors become stronger and more intense also. Increased and enhanced friendships is a real hello, one of the most delightful ups to counter the downs of this stage of life. If the Third Passage of marriage seemed like the doldrums, you're into a fresh breeze again.

The inevitable losses carry a toll you may not realize immediately. They are constant mortality-reminders. They depress the spirit. They whisper seductively, "See what's happening! Better seize life while you may!"

A necessary part of coping with the changes of middle life is to understand those changes. Sometimes that's all you really need—to understand what's happening. There is no better therapy than knowing you're not alone. Rest assured that others also feel the physical, sexual, and emotional changes you do.

One tangible way to do this is by talking to others who are experiencing mid-life too, and enduring its crises, its unique pleasures and predicaments. Here is where you reap the real benefit of good friends. Some old, some new, most valued (probably a few bores), but by and large, they form a natural, free, and very effective support group.

Building Friendships

How did Annie and Rob meet Joan and Harold, their rafting buddies? Rob would have had a hard time remembering, but Annie could tell you exactly. During a spring sale at Leadbetter's, Annie was having trouble finding a pair of pants that fit well. Joan, shopping at the same time, had the same problem, and they found themselves pawing through racks looking for each other's size as well as their own. The chance meeting developed into lunch. They hit it off famously, and when the husbands came to meet them after work, all four went out to dinner. Years later, the friendship still flourished.

Good friendships hardly ever fall into one's lap that conveniently. But one need not wait for serendipity to strike, if it at all. Good same-sex friendships can be built. Men in particular should look to developing true, solid friendships. There are four elements of an effective building plan.

1. Take Some Risks

Question: "If I were in great emotional pain or under severe pressure, to whom could I turn to unload, to talk, to reveal my inner fears?"

Wrong answer: "No one."

Best answer: "Several people (and name them)."

Friends are people you can trust to understand and keep their mouths shut if you reveal what's going on in your life. That is what we mean by risk-taking. Obviously, you must be that sort of friend in return. Every person needs at least one friend with whom he or she can risk vulnerability. "Vulnerable" means, literally, "wound-able." When you open up to another person, and that person can laugh at your pain or tell others, and that ridicule or lack of confidentiality *really* hurts. That is the sort of hurt you must risk, if the friendship is to weigh much.

But vulnerability is not a gym bag that you zip open and there it all is, hanging out. Vulnerability comes progressively to a friendship, a little at a time, with caution. As you build a friendship, therefore, open the zipper a bit, a bit wider, a bit wider. Pay heed to the way you reveal yourself and hear your friend's revelations. By taking small risks of exposure and vulnerability, you strengthen your ability to take larger ones.

2. Structure Time Together
Question: "What comes first, business or friendships?"
Wrong answer: "Business."
Best answer: "One way or another, I'll make time for friends."

We strongly recommend that friends schedule regular times of encounter. This structure is necessary if you would effectively get past the shyness, the busy-ness, and the arduous pressure of work and family that scuttle so many friendships.

The time for friends will not come spontaneously. It must be made.

3. Find a Common Bonding Experience
For Joan and Annie, it was shopping. It's how they met. They both enjoyed it. Neither of them liked to shop just for the heck of it, wasting time wandering from store to store. Both shopped with a purpose—to purchase specific things. However, neither woman minded in the least the shopping involved to find the other woman's things.

For example, on one occasion Joan was looking for a purse to match new shoes, and Annie was seeking a replacement appliance for her toaster that had just gone moccasins up. They met at the mall and helped each other shop purses and housewares. They had a great time.

Rob and Harold couldn't care less about shopping but they found common interest in golf. ("Boring!" chorused the women). You see, the two couples enjoyed a close four-way friendship, but the same-sex members also pursued friendship at a different level, one on one.

Counselors in an adolescent treatment program know the

value of bonding and may take their young clients on some grueling or demanding activity, such as rock climbing. Men and women in the Fourth Passage may prefer to forgo some of the grueling-ness in favor of comfort. How about a sport such as golf? Shopping? Taking the grandkids to the park? Attending a weekly game or event? Getting together for Pictionary™ or Trivial Pursuit™?

4. Involve God
   Question: "Does my best friend understand and appreciate my own spiritual convictions?"
   Wrong answer: "I never discussed it with him/her."
   Best answer: "It's one of our best bonding factors."
   Involving God in the process of being a friend cannot be overstated. Unfortunately, both men and women often find it difficult to introduce a spiritual aspect to what they see as basically a secular friendship. We do not suggest that your spiritual views must match your friend's. Some of the closest friends are men or women whose spiritual convictions seem at cross purposes. The important part is that each knows the other's spiritual state, and each respects the other's beliefs.
   Try to convert your friend? Maybe. Banter? Sure. Let it be? Probably. The telling cue is that you can pray with that person, talk about God's work in your life to an understanding ear . . . The spiritual dimension is an incredibly strong bond.

What About You?

Think now of the friends you have, individually and as a couple. Make two lists. On the first list, put down at least five same sex friends you enjoy spending time with as an individual:

My Individual Friends

1. _____

2. _____

3. _____

4. _____

5. _____

On the second list, name at least five couples that you and your spouse enjoy socializing with:

Our Couple Friends

1. _____

2. _____

3. _____

4. _____

5. _____

Now to the right of each name on both lists, write the amount of time you spend with each friend or each couple. Is it hours in a week, days in a month, days in a year, or a few days every few years?

For the couple friends, talk together with your spouse about the time you are spending with other couples. Circle those couples you want to spend more time with. Then decide how much more time you want with these friends and plan to do something with them very soon.

Do this same exercise individually with your first list. Make definite plans to spend more time with a special friend if you see a need. Ask yourself this question: If I were facing great pain, are there one or two friends to whom I can turn and honestly devulge what I am facing?

An unfortunate fact of life is that you are not getting any younger. Neither are your friends. Time is running out, sometimes sooner than you think.

Resolving Problems with Friends

"Mark has cancer." Annie said as she hung up the phone. Tears were beginning to flood her eyes.

"What? He's only forty-five!" Rob found himself gaping. Mark was so healthy, in such good shape. Much better than he. They hadn't seen Mark or Candy Emerson since the Emersons moved to Atlanta a few years ago. But they still kept in touch with an occasional phone call, letter, and of course the xeroxed newsletter in the Christmas card. The Emerson children were much younger than Beth Anne. Cathy, the youngest, was still in grade school.

"How?" Rob asked. "Or, I mean how bad?"

"They give him six months, a year tops."

"Did he have any symptoms?"

"Some indigestion, that's all."

"I just don't believe it. It doesn't seem right."

"I know. Candy's taking it pretty hard. It's been a real shock. The kids are, too." Her eyes poured across his face. "Rob, they're so little. It's so unfair . . ."

Annie melted down into her chair. She looked so defeated, like a sail without wind. Rob crossed to her.

"Oh, Rob, what's happening to our friends? First, Fiona and now Mark. Is it the environment or what?"

"I dunno." Rob perched on her chair arm and leaned down. Helpless to do anything more, he put his arms around her.

We have seen the verities of life compared to a long, arching footbridge across a chasm. At the far end of the bridge the babies begin their crossing on hands and knees. They learn to toddle, to walk, to run. As they come laughing across the chasm, they grow in age, reaching their prime at midspan. On this side of the bridge, dark archers are firing arrows at the approaching people. They miss the folks at the far end most of the time, for the babies are so small and so distant, the young people so active and quick. But the people slow considerably as they get older, approaching the dark side. Arrows find their mark more and more often as the happy bridge-walkers come, for not only are they bigger and slower, they are closer. They make increasingly easy targets.

No one reaches the other side.

It's no coincidence that you will start losing more and more friends as you age. Heart attacks, illnesses and just plain accidents will occur more and more frequently now. Suddenly, your mortality is very obvious as you experience your peers leaving this earth. You may have no more time than the present to resolve any difficulties within your friendships.

We highly recommend, for your peace of mind, that you make a point to resolve any and all issues between your friends now. Take a moment to think of any fences which need mending between persons you know. Think of this as you answer the following questions:

List the people who will be most missed in your life (they don't have to be friends; relatives count here also):

1. _____
2. _____
3. _____
4. _____
5. _____

Is there anyone on this list that you've needed to resolve a problem with and haven't yet? Or is there anyone on the list you always wanted to tell something to and you haven't got around to it? Fill in the following statement to see:

"I always wish I would tell _____
that _____."

"I'm sorry I've never told _____
how I really feel about him/her."

"When I hear the statement 'mend what needs mending, say what needs saying,' I think of: _____
_____
_____."

Is there a situation in which you, as a third party, could mend a rift between two friends, or help a friend patch a relationship? Jot a few words of reminder about details:

A friend of ours related the following story during a Bible study on death. "I had a friend who was killed suddenly in a mountaineering accident in California. He had small children. The death was hardest for me because we had a falling out in our relationship years before. And, I always meant to touch base again with him, let him know that I forgave him and still loved him. Now I don't have that chance and I never will. His death is tragic, but so is the loss of that relationship."

We find that persons who resolve their relationships with others handle the deaths of those other persons much better than those who did not. Forgiveness is for your benefit more than the person whom you need to forgive. Is there anyone you haven't forgiven for a past deed? Now is the time.

Examine Your Patterns of Friendships

A how-not-to-do-it story comes from a family in our neighborhood. Two generations ago, the grandmother, then twenty-two, stayed home to care for her widowed mother while her six brothers and sisters married and left. Only when the great-grandmother died did the grandmother begin her own life. She married late and bore four children. As her latter years unfolded, she and her semi-invalid husband broke their ties with friends and relatives, one by one. Grandma was a widowed recluse when her third child married. The youngest remained home and cared for her until her death.

The youngest was nearly twenty-eight when that grandmother died. After several years of wild-oat-sowing, she settled down with a good man and raised two girls. The girls went off to college. The good man died. And the pattern fell into place without a word spoken. In fact, the family's history had never even been discussed. Like her grandmother and mother before her, she began the lengthy process of cutting her ties. She didn't call friends anymore. She quit sending Christmas cards when the postage went up. Her elder sister, also widowed, became a recluse tended by daily visits from her son. Once dear friends, the two sisters never communicated anymore. The children, the cousins, communicated on the mothers' behalf.

But then this mother's world came apart. For three generations at least, the unspoken pattern had held firm. "The youngest, the caretaker, does not have permission to marry until Mom dies." And then her youngest daughter did not heed it. The daughter lives in Hawaii now, raising her family. The other kids have all made their own lives, but you see, all along, the unspoken law freed them to do so. They followed the pattern.

The mom, now seventy, sits alone in Texas, devoid of ties, still reclusive because below conscious level, she is still following that unspoken law. She likes to collect unusual stones, but she will not join a geology club. She plays solitaire, but she never goes down to the local senior center (four blocks away) to play cards with others. She will not resume ties with neighbors and friends still living in the area. She is mindlessly waiting, waiting, waiting for her daughter to come take care of her, to follow the ancient pattern.

Every family possesses an unwritten, unspoken, unthought-of code of behavior, rules passed from generation to generation. You will find it helpful, and perhaps very wise, to examine the rules that direct your family. They may be contributing to the success of your relationships. But if they are sabotaging your relationships, as is the case with the mother we just cited, they can be doing you great harm. You've nothing to lose by bringing them to light and scrutinizing them, and possibly much to gain.

The family you grew up in, of course, will wield far more influence on you than will the families you married into.

New Relationships with Your Friends

Some people cannot go back this far. If you can, at least on one side of the family, it will help.

My two sets of grandparents:

Paternal Maternal

____	____	enjoyed a wide circle of friends.

Paternal Maternal

____ ____ enjoyed a wide circle of friends.
____ ____ cultivated only a few close friends.
____ ____ had no friends that I know of in
their later years.
____ ____ attended family reunions and other
gatherings.
____ ____ kept few ties with relatives.
____ ____ belonged to special-interest clubs,
senior groups, etc.
____ ____ became more reclusive in their latter
years.
____ ____ moved out into a wider circle of
friendships.
____ ____ Other _____

My spouse's grandparents:

Paternal Maternal

____ ____ enjoyed a wide circle of friends.
____ ____ cultivated only a few close friends.
____ ____ had no friends that I know of in
their later years.
____ ____ attended family reunions and other
gatherings.
____ ____ kept few ties with relatives.
____ ____ belonged to special-interest clubs,
senior groups, etc.
____ ____ became more reclusive in their latter
years.

_____   _____   moved out into a wider circle of
                      friendships.
_____   _____   Other _____

Now consider your parents' life-styles in their latter years.
Here is where family patterns, as they relate to you, will
become most obvious.

My parents:

_____ enjoy a wide circle of friends.
_____ cultivate only a few close friends.
_____ have no friends that I know of in their later years.
_____ attend family reunions and other gatherings.
_____ keep few ties with relatives.
_____ belong to special-interest clubs, senior groups,
       etc.
_____ become more reclusive as they get older.
_____ are moving out into a wider circle of friendships.
_____ Other _____

My spouse's parents:

_____ enjoy a wide circle of friends.
_____ cultivate only a few close friends.
_____ have no friends that I know of in their later years.
_____ attend family reunions and other gatherings.
_____ keep few ties with relatives.
_____ belong to special-interest clubs, senior groups,
       etc.
_____ become more reclusive as they get older.
_____ are moving out into a wider circle of friendships.
_____ Other _____

As I get older, I find that I:

_____ enjoy a wide circle of friends.

_____ cultivate only a few close friends.

_____ have no friends to speak of.

_____ attend family reunions and other gatherings.

_____ keep few ties with relatives.

_____ belong to special-interest clubs, senior groups etc.

_____ seem to be becoming more reclusive.

_____ am actively moving out into more friendships.

_____ Other _____

As my spouse gets older, I see him or her:

_____ enjoying a wide circle of friends.

_____ cultivating only a few close friends.

_____ with no friends to speak of.

_____ attending family reunions and other gatherings.

_____ keeping few ties with relatives.

_____ belonging to special-interest clubs, senior groups, etc.

_____ seeming to be becoming more reclusive.

_____ actively moving out into more friendships.

_____ Other _____

Examine the similarities and differences carefully. Think about your aunts, uncles, and cousins. Can you see any particular patterns emerge?

In a few words, describe any pattern you detect that would help you build a comforting circle of good friends:

_____

_____

Describe any patterns that would hinder you from building that supportive circle:

_____

Do you see any pattern that governs how you interact
with relatives, in both the immediate and extended families?

Both spouses' family patterns affect your marriage. Both
have hidden agendas delivered by prior generations, and
without realizing it, you and your spouse are probably trying
to complete them. Discuss this matter with your spouse.
What do the two of you want in the way of friendships, and
how much are your old family patterns influencing your
wants?

Is compromise necessary? It may well be.

Building New Friendships

In this Fourth Passage, you at last have some time and
freedom to really work on surrounding yourself with people
you enjoy and trust. You're a shrewder judge of human nature—a gift that comes with maturity—and know better
what kind of people you like to be around and what kind of
people you don't.

Particularly, if you've been moving around quite a bit during your married life, you may find that the people on your
Christmas card list are practically strangers to you. You
haven't seen them in years. You don't know what their kids
look like anymore. And you're not retired yet, so you can't
just go travelling to renew old acquaintances. You need
good friends now, right here.

If you want to enjoy new friends and new dimensions to
life, you and your spouse may wish to join one or more
organizations that reflect your interests.

• You may have been associated with professional and service organizations such as Lions or Rotary for years. They
  welcome older newcomers, too, you know.

• What are your interests? There's a group for everyone. Car clubs for various sports car marques (MG Club, for example), horse owners' associations, hobby groups such as model railroaders and doll collectors, and activity clubs such as rockhound clubs and gourmet groups who meet in each others' homes for specially prepared meals.

"Classic John Deeres," a friend told us. "You know, those big old two-banger farm tractors from the fifties? There's a club for John Deere owners. Green and yellow shirts to match their green and yellow tractors . . . green and yellow tent marquees . . . Absolutely bilious!"

The companies for which you and your spouse work offer a broad range of possible friendships. You might wish to keep relationships in your particular department on a business basis. Friendships in the workplace should be developed with caution.

The church is an organism, not an organization, and it is there that you will probably cement lasting friendships. The church, as it was meant to be, is a body of believers of like mind, supporting and helping each other, enjoying each other, working shoulder to shoulder. Socializing, though important, is secondary to the work of the church. That makes it no less enjoyable.

In all of these organizations—and organisms—people of all ages gather. Generally speaking, the couple in the Fourth Passage does well to cultivate friendships in a spectrum of age groups. Older friends make warm friends; younger ones keep you feeling young. The wide age range also presents a wide range of opportunities to be of help to others.

Caveat Amicus

Rob Millen really didn't mean to bump into Jennifer, an attractive red-head. He was stopping by the kitchen in the church basement to get Annie's casserole dish, and, unknown to him, Jennifer was coming out the door. Bump! She apologized profusely, aflutter with embarrassment.

He apologized profusely, aflutter with amazement at how bouncy and youthful she seemed.

"You're Annie Millen's husband, right?"

"Right!"

"Say. We're putting together a hot-meals catering service for shut-ins and aged. Your wife is a wonderful organizer, and so are you. Would you two serve on my committee? We can sure use you."

Rob was all set to become just as bouncy and youthful with his *We sure would! You bet!.* He contained himself. Bouncing isn't macho. "I'll talk to Annie about it. What's your phone number?"

She told him and he wrote it on the back of one of his business cards. He gave her another card, just so she could make contact if she needed something.

With a few more bright words she hurried off. In the basement he found Annie's dish on the side table and picked up Madge's as well. Madge wasn't here this week and she lived just down the block. He or Annie could run her dish down to her.

By the time he left the church and walked around to his car, the little white Toyota was gone from the far lot.

We shouldn't have to say it, but we will anyway. There are some friendships and acquaintanceships you should avoid at all costs. You know which ones they are. Down deep, Rob knows now, too.

The Ultimate Friendship

There is one person, Lord willing, who will move when you move, go where you go, stay with you through thick and thin, and knows you better than anyone else does. Your spouse. That person cannot fill *every* friendship role totally. You still need other confidantes. But your spouse is certainly a friendship that should be cultivated as a friendship.

How deep is your friendship with your spouse? Consider these aspects of any other generalized friendship:

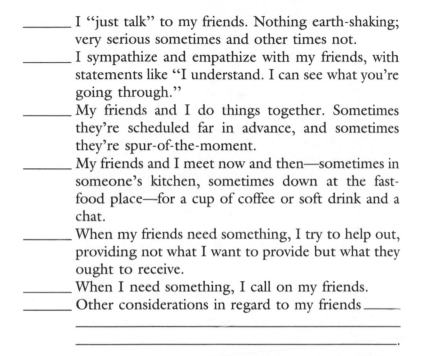

_____ I "just talk" to my friends. Nothing earth-shaking; very serious sometimes and other times not.

_____ I sympathize and empathize with my friends, with statements like "I understand. I can see what you're going through."

_____ My friends and I do things together. Sometimes they're scheduled far in advance, and sometimes they're spur-of-the-moment.

_____ My friends and I meet now and then—sometimes in someone's kitchen, sometimes down at the fast-food place—for a cup of coffee or soft drink and a chat.

_____ When my friends need something, I try to help out, providing not what I want to provide but what they ought to receive.

_____ When I need something, I call on my friends.

_____ Other considerations in regard to my friends ____

_____

_____.

How many of those items for consideration can you apply favorably to your spouse? When improvement is needed, we suggest building a genuine friendship with your spouse in exactly the same way you would build friendship with any other person. Use the four steps described above.

For example, Annie noticed how distant she and Rob had become over the years as each was involved in individual pursuits. The kids were no longer such a common bond. Likely, they never would be again.

1. Both Rob and Annie needed practice in making themselves vulnerable to each other. Annie saw no need to confide anything; Rob would take it wrongly or fail to understand. Men, she felt, can't understand like women can. Whether she was right or wrong in that, she had to begin the slow process of peeling her defenses back and baring her soul—not all at once, but increasingly so.

Rob, too, should be doing it. Perhaps he has worries or

fears about their financial future. He should share them. Should he share his growing interest in Kerri? No way. There is intimacy and there is cruelty.

2. Annie and Rob need to plan time together, just the two of them. In one way, that's easier now because the kids are older. But it's harder now, too, because Rob and Annie are so wrapped up in their separate worlds. They'll have to really work at scheduling time for each other.

3. What activity could they use for bonding? "Not a blessed thing," Rob would say. "We don't like any sports in common."

With that statement, Rob would be considering activities he and Annie are already familiar with. Annie doesn't like tennis. Rob loves it. Tennis is out. He hates going through stores. Shopping is out. They both get bored with games after awhile.

Rob and Annie would both find pleasure, though, in trying things neither of them has done before. As a random example, let's use fly-fishing. Annie never went fly-fishing. Neither did Rob. They could check out a how-to video and rent, borrow, or purchase a minimum of equipment. Avid fly-fishermen are always glad to lend equipment and even provide instruction; avid enthusiasts of any pursuit are that way. You need only find one and express interest.

The fly-fishing adventures might be fun and they might be absolute disasters to be laughed about forever after. No matter. It's the bonding. And should Rob and Annie find they enjoy fly-fishing, their lives are so much the richer.

4. Rob and Annie went to church together their whole marriage, but they were never really spiritually wedded. Sure, they belonged to the same church, sat in the same pew. "Not once," Annie could claim, "have Rob and I ever mentioned God to each other." Many, many married couples can claim that honestly.

On one of the dates they scheduled together (a la step two), Rob and Annie might each explain to the other exactly what God means to him and her. It would be enlightening for both. The discussion would also invoke step one, taking risks. Talking about spiritual matters is soul-baring at its best.

They might undertake to pray together—formal prayer on their knees in the privacy of their bedroom.

"I'd feel like an idiot," Rob might protest, "or a fanatic."

"Prayer is important, but . . ." Annie might protest.

And we would say, "Try it."

Try it.

That's what good friends do.

The Money Pit

One of the aspects of friendship that strains quickest is the tussles over money. How to spend it, save it, use it, get it. Let's look at that next.

Chapter 8

Your Financial Realities

"**M**oney." Grayson Felder wags his head. "It can make or break a marriage union. I know. My wife and I suffered massive financial reversal and it just about wrecked our lives."

Thirty years after Gray entered into an arrangement with an appliance distributor and opened a showroom, he had eight showrooms scattered across three counties in central Arizona. Then inflated Arizona land values dived to reasonable levels. The area's whole economy did a disappearing act. Home builders quit building, apartment houses stood vacant, home owners cut back and often sold at a loss. Gray Felder's business collapsed. He salvaged a little something by selling off the existing showrooms and paring his holdings to one small outlet in Gilbert, where business property rents were still low.

As his business telescoped, Gray went through the whole grieving process. He denied that he was going to have to scale back even though he saw it coming months in advance. In a literal state of shock, he rationalized that things would pick up soon although no signs said that. Denial didn't work.

He became irritable and highly critical of his wife, turning his intense anger against her (he didn't see it at the time). For six months he drifted into a state of depression and resignation. He thought it was a period of acceptance and that he was through the worst of it. Not so.

Paralyzed by depression, he was unable to act in a business capacity. Things slid downhill faster. There were days when he wouldn't answer the phone as crisis and chaos tumbled around him.

He entered a wild bargaining stage. "If I do more inside and outside the office, spend more time on God's work, somehow it will turn around." "If I offer enough sacrificial service, God will salvage my business." That lasted three months until he burned out. Finally, he ended up in true grief. Tears poured spontaneously. Deep sadness engulfed him as he admitted at last that he was going to lose it and couldn't turn it around with any amount of bargaining.

He and his wife accepted the belt-tightening that had to be done. They had to accept that their dream of financial security was lost. At fifty-five they were starting over.

We often tell couples in the Fourth Passage of marriage, "You need to come to terms with your financial state."

Those who read the book about the Third Passage, *Steadfast Love,* would claim, "I already did that, didn't I?"

"You were supposed to reach a realistic appraisal," we reply, "of where you were and where you wanted to be. You still had time then to change things. You don't anymore. You are there. You've peaked out now. And that requires grieving and resolution."

Gray and his wife may have lost their basis of financial security, but actually, they won. Throughout their marriage, Gray and his wife had substituted busy-ness for intimacy. They were solidly married to the ideal of marriage, but not really to each other. They had never completed the First Passage, let alone the Second or Third. He built the business, served on the church board, belonged to an active civic group. She raised the kids and volunteered in her church and in several service organizations. As painful and tragic as it was, that business collapse gave them the opportunity to rediscover each other, to finish what had never been finished.

What was missing from their lives all those years was genuine intimacy—knowing each other. They finally invested their time, not in business or even so much in service any more, but in each other. These days they keep their goals scaled back. Both realize that if they had finished the first few passages, they would have had no need to keep so busy. They would not have been seeking false satisfactions and false intimacies. Today they are building a happiness that will last for the rest of their lives. You can't say that about any financial investment.

Accepting Your Financial Realities

By the Fourth Passage of marriage, your financial state becomes crucial and glaringly obvious. No longer do you have the time or opportunity to greatly change it. Your challenge now is to accept and work within this reality to the best of your ability.

Originally, we covered preparation for financial retirement in the Fifth Passage of our hardback bestseller, *The Passages of Marriage* (Nashville: Thomas Nelson, 1991). Rethinking this a bit, we decided to put retirement planning in this Fourth Passage. Better yet would be for you to make certain your retirement arrangements are in place during your Second or Third Passage. All financial experts agree, the earlier you start preparing for retirement, the better. However, realistically, during the Second and Third Passages of marriage, you may be doing your best just to stay above water with economic drains such as housing, children, college for the children, and possibly aging parents.

Before you prepare for your retirement, you must take a good hard look at your current financial state and resolve any losses you feel in this arena. Take a moment now to list any and all financial and/or career dreams you had for yourself. Try to think of at least five:

1. _____

2. _____

3. _____

4. _____

5. _____

For example, one of Rob Millen's dreams was to have his own business. Another was to be financially secure—whatever that meant. Now look over your list and highlight those that have been realized or surpassed in your life to this point. Rob's dreams to be financially secure were met and surpassed at this point in his life. He could splurge a little. His income at the firm was more than adequate for this style of living. He was able to belong to a club and eat out as he wanted. And, he could drive an expensive imported car—another dream he had.

Celebrate those dreams that have come true. They only happened by some real hard work on your part. Give yourself a pat on the back.

Now for the hard part. Look at those dreams on your list that have not been realized. By this stage of your life, you may not materialize certain of your financial dreams. You must grieve their loss and resolve them totally. You can't look back now and wish things had gone differently. Now is the time to focus on the present and future. Rob had to resolve that he would never start a successful business at this stage of his life. On the plus side, he had a rewarding job that paid well.

The fact that Rob Millen liked his job is not true for some people. Middle age is a time when men and women tend to look hard at their occupation and opt for early retirement. That may be all right, except many times the problem is not their job—it's them. They find out, too late, that early retirement is not all it's cracked up to be. Strapped financially because they've taken a reduced pension to leave early and stressed because they are in a frantic pace to find something to keep their interest, they fall too easily into depression.

Instead of leaving a job, the solution may have been to try

and make that job more interesting through creative and innovative techniques.

A good technique to use, if you're sharply questioning your current job and thinking of jumping ship, is to ask yourself if you had the top job in your field in any firm anywhere, would it be any different? If you give this question a hard look, you will likely find out that any job can become routine and boring. The common denominator is you and your attitude about yourself. Look first to change yourself, before you leave your job thinking retirement or even another job will solve the problems.

Leaving your current job at this stage of life can not only be disappointing but financially disastrous. It may well behoove you to find other outlets for your stymied creativity outside of the workplace and hold out for the few years you have left. Those that frequently change jobs don't have as stable a pension as those that stay with a firm for thirty years or longer.

Planning Financially for Retirement

Many books, articles, and folders from financial institutions can help sort through the maze of available investment and income opportunities. Ideally, financial planning by the Fourth Passage of marriage should consist of fine-tuning existing plans already made in response to the current economic climate. We are not financial experts, thus we will not offer suggestions for financial retirement strategies. It's best if you consult a trusted financial adviser in this arena. If you haven't taken an active interest in your retirement, do so now!

With the onslaught of baby boomers approaching retirement, the public and private sector have turned retirement back to the individual worker. No longer can you depend absolutely on your company to provide for you after you retire. A pension plan may not be adequate to keep pace with a sluggish economy and inflation. Most experts agree that a combination of personal savings, pension plan, and personal retirement plans such as a Keogh, IRA, or 401(k) is necessary.

Nowadays, retirement is a team effort between the government, the employer, and the employee. But let's look at this team: The government is a weak member. It comes as no surprise that Social Security will be stressed as our population pyramid moves from younger to older age groups.

Now what about the employer? Companies are doing what they can, but too often benefits are being cut in times of economic hardship.

Thus, the member of the team where the most improvement can come from is you, the employee. Do whatever you can to supplement your retirement. Even a little is better than nothing. But do it now, immediately! A number of organizations have some very helpful pamphlets for this endeavor. The American Association of Retired Persons (AARP) is one good source.

Mentally Preparing for Retirement

The finances themselves are only a part of financial preparation, though. There is also the mental preparation to make in this area.

What do you envision as a retirement lifestyle? Do you want to maintain the level of income and activity you have now? Maybe move up a notch? Perhaps you'd rather seize this opportunity to downsize both lifestyle and budget. Now may be a good time to simplify your life; take it easy; reduce the housework, chores, duties, needs, and general complexities of modern existence. Set firmly in mind what you and your spouse anticipate and want.

The wise squirrel travelling around in our decision tree will stash nuts away in more than one hollow limb. The wise squirrel will also make sure it has a Plan B, should Plan A fail. Emery Wilkins, a client of ours, thought he had his finances all worked out. But being forced into early retirement, he had ten years less time to build a retirement kitty. That put a serious crimp on his future income. Emery and his wife Mabel had intended to just live in the house they had. That was Plan A. But the only bathroom was on the second floor. The house was too big to maintain comfortably should Emery or Mabel get laid up. Besides, Emery needed a bigger nest egg. So he had to shift into Plan B: sell this house, buy a much smaller, less expensive one, and dump the money into their retirement fund. Both of them hated the idea. They had to do it, though. Grief. On the other hand, it improved their immediate financial outlook. Celebration. Good-bye and hello.

Emery looked at it philosophically. "I have some friends who live in one room in a downtown hotel. I'm not going to complain about selling our family home when I've got this nice little house on Grove Street."

Many pending retirees look toward an inheritance of some sort from the previous generation. For mental peace as well as financial stability, we advise against exaggerated expectations. With inflation, longer life span, and extraordinary health care, inheritances stay within the generation longer, often dwindling as the years go by.

Emery faced what most workers face; during the First Passage of his marriage, he was making barely enough to establish himself and care for his family. Not until the Fourth Passage was he earning enough to salt away appreciable savings toward retirement. So, early retirement hit him hard. He had to mentally adjust to a much harsher reality than he would have had to, had he worked into his sixties.

Building a Mutual Dream

Mabel and Emery, though, were guilty of the most serious of retirement problems. They had never talked about it. This was the first thing we did when Mabel and Emery came to us; we sat them down knee to knee, face to face, to explain to each other their hopes and fears. You should do that too.

Here are some points to start you out. Each spouse answers individually. Compare answers and talk about compromises where compromise is necessary. Answer according to the picture you foresee during your first five years of retirement:

"We will live:

_____ in our present home."
_____ in a smaller/larger home."
_____ in a retirement home."
_____ with one of the kids."
_____ in a recreation vehicle."
_____ in a small apartment."
_____ out of the country."
_____ other—specifically _____."

"We will travel:

_____ a lot."
_____ hardly at all."
_____ now and then."

"We will engage in:

_____ a home business."
_____ no business at all."
_____ volunteer work."
_____ a part-time business or franchise."
_____ something to supplement our income."
_____ other—specifically _____."

"We have the following hobbies to occupy our time and keep us sharp: _____
_____
_____."

There are many other questions to be decided. After you complete this chapter, talk together about what you read here.

Mabel's best friend, Jeanne, planned to lease out her house and travel when they retired, only to learn that her husband was making a list of all the local fishing holes. Emery's pal Gus wanted to sell everything, live in an RV and travel all over. His wife had no intention of giving up her home. Come retirement, the couple literally ripped in half because they had never talked about it. Neither would they negotiate their dreams.

Develop Plan B

Harry reaches mandatory retirement age. His wife Henrietta did not work outside the home. They save monthly for ten years in anticipation of this time. But it's not enough. Too late they discover that social security will not cover it all. This isn't a case of bad planning, either. Even the best of planners experience a setback in states or eras with an ailing economy.

It's very easy to fall into the role of victim when this sort of thing happens. Harry and Henrietta risk losing these rich later years to bitterness. They must grieve what might have been and immediately and continuously brainstorm options. A major step in resolving sticky situations is to recognize what you can control and what you cannot. Saving regularly; Harry and Henrietta could control that. They could not control the economy, or things like the death of a spouse, a lay-off or forced retirement. Observe what you cannot control, so as to respond to it, but put it aside as a source of worry. Concern yourself rather with what you can control.

Using what you can control and manipulate, develop alternative plans that provide a workable response to those things beyond your control. It sounds basic, an idea everyone should be doing, but we've found that very few people actually do it. When problems loom large, people fumble about, fearful and confused, for solutions that might not have been hiding if they had considered them beforehand.

Harry and Henrietta decided to go to work to support themselves in their retirement. In spite of laws protecting against age discrimination, Harry could not find a job equivalent to what he had been doing. Henrietta faced entry-level work whatever she did. Still the combined income helped to offset their deficit. Now could they reduce their living cost?

The first thought was to sell their old Edwardian house. They resisted the idea vigorously. As Plan B they decided to sell some blue-chip stock they held to pay the house off. This would reduce their monthly costs considerably. Then, because living in the house was more important to them than some other niceties, they decided to limit their money for recreation, like eating out several times a week and traveling to far away places. "We've seen enough of the world," Henry said. "A trip every couple of years will do." Their lifestyle and stock ownership was something they could control. Plan B was not preferred, but it was workable. They dropped back to Plan B out of necessity. You may have to also.

No wise squirrel in a decision tree limits itself to one limb. Formulate alternative plans and research them thoroughly. This planning can be a real boost to the middle age blahs. Suddenly you have something to hold your interest and a vested interest it is—your future!

What Hinders Your Plans?

Aside from things out of your control—the economy for example—your relationship with your spouse can actually hinder your plans. How? It's just this vested interest that starts raising red flags.

Control issues. Boy, do they crop up here when it comes to planning for retirement! Persons who would swear they never had a control problem in their entire marriage find themselves saddled with them now as they mutually prepare

for retirement. Basically, couples who shared decision making and worked out control issues throughout marriage will
have the least difficulty as retirement looms.

Dwight Campbell, a retired park ranger, and his wife Alice
were driving through Beatty, Nevada, one afternoon while
on a looksee trip to find a place to live. Traffic was at a
standstill at the only stoplight in town as two dogs fought it
out. The snarling melee stopped as the larger dog rolled
over in the classic submissive position. The smaller cur stood
over the larger dog in victorious triumph.

"This is the place." Dwight announced.

They live there to this day, sipping lemonade on the porch
of their forties vintage home. They even adopted one of the
dogs as their own.

Dwight and Alice and the dogs represent two forms of
conflict. The dogs fought each other, not an issue—it was a
personal fight (as is common in the animal kingdom).
Dwight and Alice didn't fight, nor did they discuss the issue.
Dwight simply decided. His decision was powerful: Where
they would spend the rest of their life.

If Alice had disagreed, she could either make the dogfight
look tame with her anger, or she could bury the resentment
and submit to Dwight's dominance, living the rest of her
days in a very miserable fashion.

During negotiation of your retirement plans, it's wise to
keep in mind the conflict resolution skills you've acquired
from the former passages of marriage. In addition, it's wise
to consider the following methods. Each of these methods
apply not only to retirement planning, but to all the issues
hitting you during this Fourth Passage.

Decision Making

More than any other time in your marriage, you need
each other during this period to both be actively involved in
the decisions of everyday life. Talk over issues or problems,
put your heads together and come up with solutions. Two

minds are much better than one and you will more likely uncover creative remedies when you both are involved.

Identify the issue or problem together. That's easier said than done. Annie Millen certainly knew something was wrong with her marriage. But she didn't know what. When Rob and she both sat down and simply talked about it, that's when the problems began to emerge to be tagged and solved.

Second, agree on the nature of the problem. Do this without laying blame on each other. The problem is simply there, it wasn't caused by you or your spouse. Emery Wilkins' problem was his forced early retirement. It was not his fault, he didn't perform any worse on the job. It was just a matter of economics, the company was reducing overhead. Emery and Mabel quickly identified the problem as early retirement and the nature of the problem—reduced time to prepare for retirement.

Third, brainstorm solutions. Don't get locked into one at the exclusion of other, maybe better, options. Emery and Mabel decided to sell their house and move into a less expensive one. If that hadn't worked, they could always fall back on Plan B: supplement their income by one or the other going back to work, maybe still sell the house, but just rent another one until they could afford to buy.

Flexibility

At this stage of the game, you must avoid getting locked into one pattern of living. Flexibility in decision making: the man who has made all the family decisions up to this point is letting the wife make some of the decisions now. And flexibility in roles:

One man described to us how he always hated leaving his wife and children and going to work everyday. He was a homebody at heart.

He liked to putter around the house, bake bread, cook meals, and be with his children. But he grew up in the era of traditions—it was the man's job to go off to a job and the woman's to stay home.

After their children left home, his wife returned to college —pursuing a dream of hers to get her PhD in Anthropology. He thinks it's great. He's retired and now a house husband. She is working at the university and publishing papers in her field.

She speaks glowingly of her husband. "Andrew is so thoughtful. He delights in surprising me with a new gourmet treat each night. I don't think I've ever seen him happier. He gets a real kick when our grandchildren come to visit."

Andrew interjects, "It's not like I'm waiting for Madge to come home every night. I do a lot. At first, I thought puttering around the house would be enough. It wasn't. That was a difficult period. Then, I realized that I didn't need Madge to really enjoy my retirement. I could by myself. So I started traveling alone. We do some trips together too, but I don't make her schedule my criteria. I also volunteer at the local high school in the vocational education department. Now more than ever I feel I am doing something useful in life."

Too often, couples get locked into one pattern, one routine. When the husband retires, the wife follows suit and they both live out retirement in the traditional sense. In our modern culture, the wife may just be gearing up in her career by the time the husband is winding down. She's not prepared mentally or financially to stop.

That can be a source of resentment and conflict between a couple. Why follow a standard prescription for life dictated by society? Be flexible, follow your hearts, and roll with the flow.

Constantly Look at Priorities

Your time is precious now, you are approaching the sunset years of your life. Don't waste it on activities you have little interest in. Throw obligation out the door. The only obligations you have are to God, to yourself, and to each other. To often we think we should devote our time to this well-deserving cause because it's the godly thing to do.

What is the godly thing? Who knows better than the Lord? No one on earth, no matter how much propaganda they feed you, knows what God's plan is for you. Better to follow your own heart. Learn to say "no" more often. (Much, much harder than saying "yes".)

Is it necessary to send out this many Christmas cards this year? Do you have to chair the Church Board, the Garden Club, and the Lion's Club? Take a good hard look at these commitments before they get out of hand. They can be sources of unnecessary stress as we discussed in Chapter Two.

One simple way to do this is to fill out the following list. List those items that take up the most of your time near the top. We call this a reality list:

Reality List - Things That Take Up My Time:

1. _____
2. _____
3. _____
4. _____
5. _____
6. _____
7. _____
8. _____
9. _____
10. _____

Now make a second list, reordering the items to match where you most like your time to go. We call this a dream list:

Dream List - Things I Want to Spend My Time On:

1. _____
2. _____

3. _____

4. _____

5. _____

6. _____

7. _____

8. _____

9. _____

10. _____

Annie Warden Millen did this exercise and found out she really wanted her time to go more on her marriage than the plethora of volunteer organizations she served on.

Try to say "no" to those time-eating activities that are at the top of the Reality List. Take control of your life and move more towards your Dream List.

This priority examining is extremely valuable when planning for retirement. Hopefully by retirement you can move towards living entirely within your Dream List. Your time is your own as they say. You have choices then, no more eight-to-five job. Now, before retirement, start gearing yourself in that direction. Spend time on the things that matter to you in your life and not on the others. One person put it this way: "Do the things that are first priority first and the things that are second priority not at all."

That sounds extremist, but it's really not. Our society is so stressful and demanding, just like a two-year-old, that we have a bunch of first priorities and a bunch of lower priorities. You are only one person, you can only do so much—the first priorities.

For example, the standard of housecleaning has dropped significantly as women have entered the workforce in throes. Why still live under your mother's ideal? A clean house is not necessarily a happy one.

Roll with the Punches

We've said over and over that life is full of gains and losses, peaks and valleys, ups and downs. All the mid-life changes we've discussed so far create a spectrum of these ups and downs. You must accept them as a fact of life and anticipate that your moods will swing just as far on the spectrum. The stress put on your marriage will also produce a certain amount of ups and downs. One day you'll be lavishing in marital bliss, the next week at each other's throats over some problem. Maybe it won't be this graphic, but the swings will occur.

Rob Millen couldn't understand the change in Annie and he wasn't sure he liked it. She had taken a sudden intense interest his hobbies—like sports. Somehow, she managed to get tickets to the big football game and gave them to him as a surprise. Even more surprising, she wanted to go with him. He was starting to feel a little smothered by Annie's involvement in his interests.

Along with the up of concentrating on their relationship, Annie was bringing out issues within Rob that caused strife and conflict between them. Through therapy, we got them to see that this was okay. As you stir things up, the water is going to get mucky, some ugly things might rear their head. That's natural, accept it. This is easier to accept if you've built a support system for each other.

Mutual Support

This Fourth Passage marks an opportunity for greater intimacy and togetherness between the two of you as we've mentioned before. As the responsibilities slowly trickle away (children, your parents, your career), time becomes your own and you truly can rediscover each other again. It's just the two of you at the dinner table now. You can even enjoy a romantic candlelit dinner complete with china and cloth napkins without interruption.

Instead of looking away from each other to outside diver-
sions, gaze lovingly into each other's eyes. Each of you is
going through the stresses of midlife now and you need the
support from the other through all the emotional, physical,
and mental hassles. Comfort and caring are key words. Nur-
ture each other. Look to your relationship as a major advantage in your life and foster it, help it grow. Give yourselves a
new reason to be together.

Chapter 9

The New Contract

*A*s you move through the Fourth Passage of marriage, profound changes occur in your life, much of which we discussed in the previous chapters. Together or singly, these changes alter circumstances so much in your marriage that you need new reasons to stay married. Too, some of the old reasons you married have died, or, in the case of the children, moved out.

Maybe you never initiated a marriage contract before. It's not too late to do one now. Or perhaps you both assumed an unspoken marriage contract when you stated your vows. That too is out-of-date at this point in your lives together. Your lives have changed too much for the old contract to work well.

Most therapists agree that journaling (a form of writing down thoughts) is extremely valuable. Somehow when the thoughts are pulled out from your mind and put down on paper, the process becomes therapeutic as the thoughts and feelings from your inner self reveal themselves to be resolved. In fact, some clients are downright shocked at the intensity of their feelings when they write them down. A marriage contract, written out, is equally as revealing.

Writing something down is not only therapeutic but practical as well. We've recommended letter writing as an effective means of communication throughout this book. A written marriage contract is another form of communication—communication between the both of you at the very deepest level. In this contract you bring your needs and wants into the open and formalize their accomplishment.

By contrast, if left unspoken, these needs can actually prevent a marriage from progressing into the next passage. To the extreme, unspoken needs can be disastrous to your marriage. Take, for example, a client of ours, Edith Simmons. During her Fourth Passage of marriage, she could not have sexual intercourse with her husband. Her doctors sent her to us when they could find nothing wrong medically. Briefly, her history was this: During her First Passage of marriage, she quit college to raise her children and keep the house in order. Her unspoken contract was that she would return to school and get her degree once the kids were out of school and on their own.

Along comes the Fourth Passage. The kids were gone. Except that every time she attempted to restart college, her husband always came up with some reason why she should wait longer—money, timing, whatever. He always had one reason or another.

Problems started in the bedroom when her vagina literally became so rigid her husband couldn't enter during intercourse. Since she felt her husband was violating her unspoken contract—to return to school now that the kids were gone—her body shut down in protest.

Literally.

Never underestimate the power of the unknown. If you are coveting any secret contracts, bring them out in the open now before they cause any problems.

When we think of marital contracts, we commonly associate them with business deals between the partners to protect one or the other financially in case of a breakup. You may even have such a contract. That's fine.

But the contract we're speaking of here is very different. It is a formalized agreement between the two of you to strengthen your marriage and to fulfill each other's needs. By contrast, then, it helps prevent a breakup.

Page 162 is an example of what such a contract could look like. Use it as a very general guide when you draft your own individual marital contract. Modify the categories to suit your own unique relationship. Keep this contract in a special place and make a commitment to periodically review and update it, especially if there have been any major changes in your life.

The Contract Work

Before you actually sit down and write out your contract, you must do a lot of introspection. Think about what would go into a renewal of your own contract at this stage of your marriage, whether you've actually reached the Fourth Passage or not. It's fun to project the future, so long as you realize it's all projection. For example, what are the new priorities and needs in your marriage? What problems need attention?

Robert Hemfelt discusses an example of this phenomenon. "It's sad. This person's parents were both terrified of death. Neither of them ever made peace with it, even though both of them met a lingering death due to disease. This person, who is forty-eight now, never made peace with it either. Now he's left his wife of thirty years. He's certain he doesn't love her anymore. He's out seeking someone younger. Actually, it has nothing to do with her or with love. He's running away from death, not marriage. He's afraid of getting old."

This man's situation is not all that uncommon. People who have not yet come to terms with their own mortality seek some way to maintain the fiction that they're not old yet. And the more cold reality closes in, the more desperate they become.

The new contract then must have an underlying theme of survival and rational thought about your lives and the changes bombarding you. The new contract should repre-

THE MARRIAGE CONTRACT
(Fourth Passage)

1. Statement of your commitment to the relationship and to the marriage.
2. A promise of fidelity.
3. Statement of positive affirmations of each other; at least one attribute you admire and appreciate in the other person.
4. Acknowledgement of your roles as examples to the younger generations and the responsibility to share your successes and failures with them (as a marital team).
5. Acknowledgement of the inevitable changes and losses happening to each of you at this stage of your life.
   a. Sexually
   b. Emotionally
   c. Physically
   d. Mentally
6. Ways to cope with and take great advantage of those changes (specific and general).
7. Acknowledgement of any hidden agendas or dysfunctions.
8. Ways to resolve these dysfunctions.
9. Ways to build intimacy (specific and general).
10. Details of everyday life (date nights, vacations, household roles) and ways to accomplish these details (negotiation with give and take).
11. Commitment to renew marriage contract periodically (anniversaries are a convenient time).

sent the premise: "We will do whatever must be done to make it to the end."

Rob and Annie Millen needed just such a contract. They worked with us to draft a new contract for their marriage. (Annie's father Carl, an old-fashioned man unaccustomed to this sort of thing, took a dim view of her efforts. "You made a covenant pact at your wedding. So you honor it. Period. Why a new contract all of a sudden?"

"Because, Pop," replied Annie patiently, "details of the old one aren't working for us anymore. This is damage control now.")

First and foremost their broad strokes included a paragraph or two vowing they would both do anything necessary to keep the union from dissolving. That was their statement of commitment to each other. They renewed the exact pledges they had made before God years ago on their wedding day.

You too should begin the contract with these renewed wedding vows. Reaffirm your commitment to each other now:

_____

_____

_____

The next general part of the contract required Annie and Rob to make a pledge of fidelity to each other, not just physically but mentally as well. You'll remember that Rob fantasized about a younger woman, Kerri, at their church. We didn't recommend he tell Annie about this; there would be no benefit from it, and Annie just might blow his fantasy out of proportion. Rather, by making his pledge of fidelity to Annie in writing, he helped stall those thoughts from becoming action. You can believe he was thinking hard when he made the statement of commitment, too.

Now, you too, should make some sort of promise not to stray on your mate. Remember how very tempting this is during this stage of life. Acknowledge that temptation exists and you will do whatever is necessary to resist that temptation:

I promise to: _____

_____

_____.

Maybe your statement of fidelity can only be: "I will do whatever is necessary to be faithful to you in thought and deed for the next year (or maybe just the next six months)." Commit to what you can abide by, what you feel comfortable with. When you update the contract, you can extend that commitment.

A word here about honesty. It is tempting—no, even expedient—to say what you think your spouse wants to hear. You do want to keep peace, so you use flowery words. Words of eternal promise. Both of you must resist that urge. Keep it practical, and above all, keep it a true reflection of reality.

Another general part of the contract concerns your role in building each other up, stroking the positive qualities. Take a moment to think of all the good things you admire and appreciate about each other. Be truthful. Perhaps the wife can say, "I admire how steadfast you are, you have provided a secure and comfortable marriage for me." The husband may state, "I appreciate how well you raised our children. Their success today is in part because of the nurturing environment you gave them."

If you can't think of anything positive to say about your spouse, look again. Even the smallest trait can be worth mentioning. Annie couldn't find any in Rob right away. We helped her see through her negative filter.

"I'm extremely bitter about my past life with Rob. In essence, he's been emotionally unavailable to me for most of our marriage."

"Fine. And, you need to work on grieving and resolving this bitterness," we answered. "But, in this contract, you're looking ahead, not behind. What do you admire about him today?"

"Well . . ." she began, wrinkling her brow. "He's willing to go through counseling with me. He didn't just leave. And, he didn't make me come alone."

"Okay, so put down that you admire his courage and commitment to work on your relationship. That's a positive trait of his you appreciate right now."

Now, think of the positive things you admire about your

spouse. Try to put down at least three. If you can think of more, great:

1.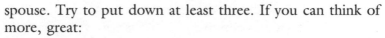

2. _____

3. _____

Rob and Annie knew the responsibility they held as role models for the generations coming up. That realization was a turning point for Annie, you'll recall. Thus, right in the contract, in writing, they reminded themselves that they served as these role models.

Susan Hemfelt puts this another way: "A couple in their Fourth Passage should consider serving as spiritual mentors to a younger couple. This is a vital role in our age of easy divorce and broken families. Share what you did wrong, so they won't make the same mistakes. If something worked, ᶜhare it also, just like you do a good recipe."

Carl and Bess Warden did this merely by being living examples of a healthy marriage. People gravitated toward them ʰoth for marital advice, even Beth Anne's new husband Alan. "Forewarned is forearmed, I always say." Carl stated many times to the younger folks, "If Bess and I knew half of what we know now, we could have avoided many a close call. Guess we were just lucky."

Lucky and fortunate, but not by chance. Bess and Carl Warden worked earnestly at their marriage every day. It was that important to them.

You may wish to formally acknowledge that you and your partner serve as role models for the generations coming up, and conduct your marriage accordingly:

_____

_____

Rob and Annie's broad overview covering these major items took about a page. For the next page and a half, they defined the narrow strokes, the details they planned to make into a formal part of their vows to each other.

Look over items five through ten of the marriage contract on page 162. Review the chapters on inevitable losses and

good-byes during this passage. Put down the changes you
both feel and see in yourselves. Then, list the ways that you
plan to cope or even take advantage of these changes. Maybe
all you can say is that you will commiserate with each other.
That's a start, a good start. You are becoming listeners.

Assuming for the moment that you have never built a
contract of this sort in the past, let's look at items five
through ten in detail.

ITEM 5: Acknowledgement of the inevitable changes and losses happening to each of you at this stage of your life.

You already mulled these in prior chapters of this book.
They should also be acknowledged in the contract itself. The
changes and losses represent the new you, the new base of
capabilities from which you can expect to operate from here
on. *Please note: Not all change represents loss.* Here you
should catalogue also the positive changes your life together
has provided. The positive alterations are just as telling as
any negative ones. Emphasize and enhance those positive
changes!

a. Sexually:
Average frequency of intercourse during the last two
years:

_____

Changes and limitations in methods, positions (example:
hip or shoulder arthritis now limits movement):

_____

_____

_____

Other changes over the last ten years (don't forget to
mention positive changes; longer foreplay, better satisfaction, and such):

_____

_____

_____

b. Emotionally:

What emotional high points and satisfactions that you have enjoyed in the past do you want to preserve or repeat for the remainder of your union? Some, such as the marriage of a child (we hope!) will not be repeatable. Look more to repeatable ones here—an especially happy anniversary celebration, pleasant times together in an activity, a special time of emotional sharing):

_____

_____

_____

What low points do you want to avoid in the future? As you mention them, also think about the reasons they were made low. What went sour? What actions should you avoid?

_____

_____

What changes has time wrought in your and your spouse's emotional responses to each other and to life (good and bad)? For example, are emotional responses more measured, wilder, balanced, thought about more, remembered better or worse . . . ? Examine the gamut:

_____

_____

_____

c. Physically:

This is probably the easiest one because physical change is right there. Remember the positive changes, too. Catalogue the changes each of you has experienced in two categories: Reversible (something correctable through medical intervention, for example) and irreversible:

_____

_____

_____

_____

_____

d. Mentally:

You've both changed your mental outlook drastically through the years. Part of that change was wrought by age, and another part was created by each other. You have been each other's greatest influence. What changes that you can think of will influence your future years together?

_____

_____

_____

ITEM 6. Ways to cope with and take great advantage of those changes (specific and general):

a. Sexual changes:

Using give-and-take, each of you discuss how the changes work both for and against a satisfying sexual relationship. (An example:

He: I take longer to reach the top and sometimes I fold in the middle. I need you to be patient with me and work with me to achieve fulfillment.

She: You don't know how wearisome it is to constantly try to figure out how to coax a good performance that doesn't fold. Sometimes I'm not satisfied.

He: Let's extend foreplay and please you first.

She: Then I'll work with you.

Both: Not all the time, or we'll lose spontaneity. But often.)

How can you use the changes you listed above to enhance your sexual relationship? In the contract, specifically commit to the ways you come up with:

_____

_____

_____

b. Emotional changes:

Look at the changes you listed above. Now in your contract, commit to ways in which you can minimize the negative changes and maximize the positive ones. This one takes some hard, eye-to-eye discussion. *No fair making comments intended to be hurtful, and no fair avoiding comments because they're uncomfortable.*

We can each help the other emotionally by:

_____

_____

_____

The husband can help the wife in these ways:

_____

_____

The wife can help the husband in these ways:

_____

_____

c. Physical changes:

Let us assume for example that arthritis prevents the wife from easily opening jars. The husband could write a contract promise that he'll open jars for her. That's pretty nit-picky.

Rather, as you write contract observations related to physical changes, we suggest you observe general needs and make promises to fill them as much as possible. In the example above, the wife could simply write, "I need help sometimes with things requiring a strong grip." The husband's response: "I will help you with problem situations your grip causes."

The wife's special needs:

_____

_____

_____

The husband's response(s):

_____

_____

The husband's special needs:

_____

_____

_____

The wife's response(s):

_____

_____

d. Mental changes:
   There is no cookbook contract statement for this topic. Look at the changes you listed above. What changes in your future life together can best minimize bad and maximize good? Brainstorm on this one—no thought too goofy, no mental stone unturned. Make a contract statement to reflect your mutual thoughts. When thinking about future mental acuities and changes, you may wish to look at your parents and grandparents. How are their mental attributes changing with age? How can you either improve upon their example in your own life, or imitate their example?

_____

_____

_____

ITEM 7. *Acknowledgement of any hidden agendas or dysfunctions.*

   You've been doing this pretty much throughout the book. You have become aware of the strange little surprises surfacing lately; or at least, you are aware such things exist. Hidden agendas, remember, need not be damaging to the spouses or the union. Harmless and beneficial hidden agendas are best left unrecognized. Why mess up a good thing? Only if they are malignant need you pay them attention.
   What patterns did you each grow up with? What were your parents' and grandparents' strengths and weaknesses? What were their mistakes? What misfortunes befell them? Now brainstorm again, the two of you, eye-to-eye. Do you see any "coincidental" similarities in your own marriage? Patterns you're repeating?

_____

_____

_____

What startling changes in attitude, behavior, or expectations has each of you experienced lately? Speculate on how some hidden agenda could have caused that (pure speculation; neither of you is saying, "This is definitely so-and-so at work." You're saying, "It could possibly be this-or-that at work"):

ITEM 8. Ways to resolve these agenda problems and dysfunctions.

How will you deal with what you found out above? Write down a couple of ways you can meet the problems and resolve them. This again will take some major brainstorming, because no couple's past can be fitted easily into a fill-in-the-blank solution.

ITEM 9. Ways to build intimacy (specific and general).

a. First, define "intimacy."
Wife: My idea of improved intimacy is:

Husband: My idea of improved intimacy is:

Our idea of improved intimacy:
Intimacy exists on many levels—sexual, emotional, etc. At all those levels, improving intimacy means getting to know the other person better, and from there to respond better to meet each other's needs.

Don't depend on our definition as "the right one." Your definitions are even more relevant because those definitions reflect your specific needs. Talk together about the definitions you framed. Talk about your needs and desires. What more do you want from your spouse as regards intimacy?

Now, based on that discussion, write a couple of promises and suggestions in each of these categories:

a. General ways the husband can enhance intimacy (come home from work a few minutes earlier, videotape the news so you can both talk over dinner . . .):

_____

_____

b. General ways the wife can enhance intimacy (avoid letting work topics monopolize time spent talking, videotape the news . . .):

_____

_____

c. Specific things the wife would like from her man:

_____

_____

_____

d. Specific things the husband would like from his woman:

_____

_____

_____

ITEM 10. Details of everyday life (date nights, vacations, household roles) and ways to accomplish these details (negotiation with give and take).

So often, the best of intentions get smothered not by major catastrophes but by big piles of little things. You two really do want to get together as a couple frequently, but the bridge club, overtime at work, his volunteer work with the fire department, her volunteer work at the library, the kids and grandkids—time together just drizzles away, banished by "important" things.

Here's where you can get very definitive and nit-picky, to excellent effect. This is the fine-tuning that will structure in time together so that it doesn't get edged out by all those other things. Here's the contract item you really do want to engrave in stone. Make it a priority. You need this item above all else, because your union really is the most important thing you can be tending.

a. Dating:
We commit to this vacation in the next year, just the two of us:

_____

_____

We commit to a date night once weekly, the two of us (the nature of the date to remain flexible), on:

_____

We commit to this activity, to be undertaken together, over the next year:

_____

b. Growth:
We commit to learning this new sport, craft, or activity together during the next year:

_____

c. Household Roles and Duties:
    "We're both busy. In the past, household duties fell into line by hit or miss. Now we're going to delegate. This will help both of us accomplish more of what we want to do, and ideally will also improve intimacy and reduce frustration."
    Putting it in black and white will resolve a lot of misunderstanding later ("But I thought you said . . ."). If you want to switch off chores, you might say "He on even numbered months, she on odd" or something. Who is responsible for:
Picking up around the house, morning or evening:

_____

Laundry and folding, putting away:

_____

Ironing and mending:

_____

Mopping, vacuuming, and dusting:

_____

Cleaning the bathroom:

_____

Dishes after supper:

_____

Taking out the garbage:

_____

Handling the recycling:

_____

Watering and tending indoor plants, pets:

_____

Watering and tending outdoor plants, pets:

_____

Tending the lawn—mow, rake, whatever:

_____

Tending the garden:

_____

Putting the garage/woodshed/carport back in order periodically:

_____

How often?:

_____

Maintaining tools, appliances:

_____

Preparing meals:
breakfast_____
lunch_____
dinner_____
potluck contributions to suppers you both attend:

_____

holidays and special occasions: _____
extra baking or cooking items: _____

Listing the major issues that really needed work was easy for Rob and Annie. They could come up with a grocery list of problems. Harder was stating ways to address those problems. They could only come up with one: "Go through counseling." That was a good one for them because it reinforced their commitment to make their marriage work whatever it would take. (Remember, also, this is the underlying theme of the entire contract.)

One problem that was detrimental to their further progress in counseling was Rob's reaction to Annie's attempts of being involved in his interests. The more Annie tried to be an active participant, the more Rob pulled away from her.

"Was there anytime in your life that you felt trapped—just like a caged animal?" we asked him.

"I'm not sure. Let's see . . . I don't know about trapped, but I felt suffocated, restrained you might say, when Beth Anne was little. Annie and I suddenly couldn't go anywhere or do anything without the baby. It got to be that the only time I could have any freedom was if I went alone or with some of the guys. I guess after that, I always spent whatever free time I had with my friends and not with Annie. Do you think that's why I feel the way I do now?"

"Maybe," we answered. "Maybe deep down you're afraid if you let Annie in on your interests, you'll somehow be giving up some of your freedom." After many, many sessions and lots of talking between the two of them, Rob was able to enjoy some activities with Annie without feeling threatened.

However, Annie also had to change. In the beginning, with Beth Anne's exodus, she tended to substitute time with Rob for the void left by the empty nest. First and foremost she had to grieve and resolve the loss of her child. Then she had to rebuild her personal identity. To date, her happiness and self-worth had been defined by her role as a wife and/or mother. At least one of these was missing and she was hanging on for dear life to the only one left—her husband. She had to let up a little and she had to build another support—herself. Eventually Annie was able to give Rob more space as she started feeling more sure of herself.

During this Fourth Passage as the two of you have increasing free time on your hands, the tendency is to spend
all that free time together. It's comfortable, secure and easy
—built-in entertainment. Too much togetherness, however,
can be just as detrimental to a relationship as too little. Be
aware of depending on each other for your total happiness
and entertainment. There will come a day when the other
won't be around and you could be left devastated if you
haven't worked on your personal identity and happiness.

Susan Hemfelt's parents have a workable arrangement as
they approach the Fifth Passage. They enjoy at least one
hobby together and at least one hobby on their own. Susan's
dad builds model railroads and tinkers with electric trains.
Susan's mom plays bridge a lot, her dad doesn't. Together
they take walks and vacations.

"It's an arrangement that has worked well for them," Susan explains, "They each have their own pursuits and interests. And, then they have things they like to do together. It's
a delicate balance that every couple approaching retirement
must make."

If you find any issues too big to handle or too complicated
to sort out as you work through this Fourth Passage and the
exercise of writing a new contract, seek help—professional
or otherwise. A marriage counselor, a pastor, a trusted
friend.

Items nine and ten are fun. Here's where you get to plan
great things together and rejoice in being a couple. Go back
through the sections of this book regarding romance, memories and laughter, and your history together. Your particular situation is unique. What specific items might you write
into a new contract to promote romance over the next years?
What exactly can both of you do to avoid taking each other
for granted?

Think about your history. What can you do to both
deepen and transmit your family history and traditions?
Write it all into the contract.

And there Annie hit a snag. "It's all very nice to talk

about history and laughter and such. But so many of my memories are flat. Rob doing his thing, ignoring me. Some of our best years are lost. We should have been together, enjoying those years, and we were essentially estranged. Emotionally, I mean. I'm very bitter about that."

Annie was right. Much had been lost. She had to sit down and work through grief and forgiveness before she could complete her new contract. You may have to as well. Necessary as they are, these struggles of grieving and forgiveness are never easy. But they are as much a part of your history as the laughter. And properly and completely accomplished, they strengthen the bond as much as do laughter and good nature.

A very useful and fun activity at this stage is to work together organizing photos, films, and videos. It can be a challenging memory game and real romance igniter. Make sure your family history is in good shape for the generations to come. A father of a friend of ours wrote his autobiography. It may not be a bestseller, but she will always have the family history in a succinct and readable format.

Now, work out the fine points, the give and take, the details. What do you want from marriage now? How can you and your spouse work together to attain it?
What we want:

_____

_____

What we must do:

_____

_____

As Susan Hemfelt says, "Reassess where you are today, where you want to be tomorrow, and how you'll get there. Put down your game plan and then use it on the playing field."

The Bottom Line

The bottom line of your contract is the same bottom line of any contract: two entities working together to achieve a

common goal. The antithesis of dysfunction, in marriage as
in anything else, is mutual aid, as each helps the other satisfy
needs and complete the necessary tasks of each passage of
marriage.

It is not necessary that all parties agree on the same
agenda in the contract. That's what the contracting process
is all about. You may well find that each of you have totally
different agendas and priorities for your relationship. Matching or meshing diverse agendas in which all parties win is
just as successful as identical agendas and maybe even better.

That's what negotiation is all about. Giving something so
that you get something in return. One result of clear communication and honest contract negotiation like this is improved intimacy—a goal of any passage marriage. You know
each other better, understand each other better, and appreciate each other better. You can better grasp what makes
your marriage tick. You can see the harmful influences and
work out ways together to combat these influences. You can
see the healthy, positive influences and capitalize on those
influences. Just the act of creating a mutually advantageous
contract can bind you together more securely. And that's
what we all want.

Have You Completed the Fourth Passage?

R ob Millen watched that cute little Kerri jog off across the churchyard. She had slipped out of her high heels and left them on the grass outside the sanctuary doors. Now, worship service over, and the sun shining bright, she was off to get her daughter from Kids' Church.

Rob picked up one of the shoes, a three-inch pump. He glanced at the lining. Kerri's feet were smaller than Annie's. Youth, liveliness, beauty—Kerri had it all.

But there was the marriage contract. Sure, Rob honored contracts. He'd been doing so his whole life. Could he violate this one? Probably. Let's be honest. The marriage contract he and Annie hammered out, for all its cutesy meanings, was unenforceable. No teeth. No lawsuit, no federal investigation, no time in the slammer—so what if he broke it?

The contract he'd made before God on his wedding day: now that was the one. Break that one at your peril. Rob didn't fear much, but he feared the Lord who had provided his salvation. Not just respect. Not just warm fuzzy feelings. Fear.

And look at Annie, giving this marriage everything she had. She delivered ultimatums (or is the plural "ultimata?"). She cajoled Rob into counseling. She was making major changes herself, in an effort to be a more responsive wife.

When Annie put her mind to something, she did it. You had to give her that.

Rob thought of the stale old joke:

Husband to forty-year-old wife: "I think I'll trade my forty in on two twenties."

Wife in response: "Forget it, Bub. You're no longer wired for 220."

Prove his youth? Hah. That tennis tourney proved all he had to know about his youth. And what was the pastor's message today? "As you sow, so shall you reap." Sow wild oats with Kerri or somebody, and reap misery, eventually. Reap loneliness in old age, a loss of everything if the new love found somebody better.

Annie was determined to make the marriage work. Rob would follow her lead and help her make the marriage work.

It was his best bet for a comforting old age. It was his only choice, where God was concerned.

Kerri disappeared into the classroom building. The door closed behind her.

Rob dropped the shoe beside its mate and walked out to the car to wait for Annie.

The Home Stretch?

If you have been married more than thirty years, you know that this is a time of either renewal or alienation. Intimacy involves opening up to each other, becoming vulnerable. It also requires learning new things about each other. That's what this Fourth Passage is all about: the ups and downs, letting go of the old things and embracing the new things.

How well have you done this? Take the following self-test to evaluate your progress through this passage of marriage. We invite you to xerox the questions for your spouse. Try to do the test individually and then discuss your results together, adjusting where you think you need to. If you haven't been married more than thirty years, this test may indicate some areas where you need to invigorate your marriage now. As Carl Warden said in the last chapter, "Forewarned is forearmed."

Our questions are grouped under the specific tasks we've discussed in this book. Simply check those statements that apply to your particular marital situation. Drs. Debi and Brian Newman use these questions to evaluate a couple that comes to them for help. You, too, can evaluate your marriage's progress.

Task One: Combat the Crisis of This Passage

_____ "I have made a decision to do everything I can to build a strong healthy marriage even after all these years."

_____ "I recognize the value of a long-lasting marriage."

_____ "I am not an active participant of the blame cycle, meaning I take responsibility for what I bring to my marriage."

_____ "We have successfully accomplished the tasks of the previous passages."

_____ "Even after a number of years together, I realize that growing marriages need effort and that we still need time alone together."

_____ "We share our thoughts, feelings, joys, and hurts with each other on a regular basis."

_____ "If there is something about my spouse that really troubles me, I can share it openly with him/her without she/he overreacting."

_____ "Our marriage is not characterized by excessive fighting or excessive non-fighting. We voice our disagreements and talk about them, using conflict resolution skills we've developed over our years together."

_____ "We lean on each other during crises."

_____ "We do not have excessive stressors in our marriage."

_____ "We meet each other's needs through give and take."

_____ "We have forgiven each other for the past mistakes and hurts in our marriage."

_____ "We have a growing, dynamic marriage that includes peaks and valleys."

_____ "My spouse is one of my greatest supporters during times of crises."

_____ "I look forward to many more years with my spouse in a relationship marked by love and harmony."

Should you find that you cannot check most, if not all, of the above statements, your marriage may not have fulfilled the requirements of this first task. Look sharply at those statements that you or your spouse couldn't check. Are there any patterns? Is support lacking in your relationship, especially during crises? How about conflict? Have you worked out control issues in your relationship? You might want to review the first two chapters of this book for insights on where you can improve things a bit under this task.

Task Two: Reestablish Intimacy

_____ "We maintain an intimate sexual relationship."

1. _____ "We are able to openly discuss sexual intimacy."

2. _____ "I am satisfied with the way sexual intimacy is initiated in our relationship."

3. _____ "I am satisfied with the frequency of our sexual experiences."

4. _____ "I enjoy the length of time we experience sexual pleasure."

5. _____ "I appreciate the setting and atmosphere of our sexual times together."

6. _____ "I am satisfied with the nature and variety of our love play."

7._____ "Overall I am very satisfied with our sexual relationship."

_____ "We freely express our affection for one another in words and actions."

_____ "When I have good news, the first person I want to tell is my spouse."

_____ "My partner is a real comfort in times of grief."

_____ "After a fight, we feel closer to each other."

_____ "I don't feel my spouse cages me in."

_____ "I enjoy (or look forward to) the extra time we will spend together in retirement."

_____ "My mate is truly my best friend."

_____ "We still enjoy holding hands and looking into each other's eyes even after all these years."

_____ "We often reflect back on our years together and enjoy these memories together."

_____ "I don't feel a sense of ending in our marriage. Rather, I feel like our marriage is just beginning to take on a new dimension."

_____ "I still try to find special ways to romantically surprise my spouse."

_____ "My most painful event this past month was:

_____.

My spouse's most painful event this past month was: _____."

_____ "We agreed on the above answers."

_____ "I feel we have a strong, growing marriage."

How about intimacy in your marriage? Is it there? Is it growing? If you answered most of the above questions, intimacy is probably a real bonus of your relationship in this passage. Consider yourself fortunate, for intimacy is the hardest feeling to maintain.

Conversely, if you couldn't check most of the above statements, your relationship could use some intimacy building. Try some of the exercises we mentioned in Chapter Three. Look for small ways to rekindle the romance in your lives.

Near the close of work one day, Annie Warden Millen showed up at Rob's office with a picnic hamper. They enjoyed dinner *al fresco* down by a subdivision on the reservoir that Rob had to go inspect anyway.

For the first time ever, Rob took Annie along when he went golfing. She didn't try to play. She drove the cart and kept score and praised his drives and laughed along with him at the ball that bounced off two trees before landing on the green. He enjoyed the round immensely.

Rob, one morning at breakfast, handed Annie a list. "Here's a list of the things you'll need to take. Meet me at the airport at five."

She stared at the innocuous looking piece of paper. "The airport . . . I have an appointment with the hairdresser for four-thirty, Rob. And tomorrow morning—"

"I canceled your appointments for tomorrow," he interrupted. "Five. Don't be late." With a peck on the cheek, out he went.

Annie stared at the list. Swimming suit. Shorts. Stocking cap. Mittens. Cocktail dress. Mostly summer clothes . . . And there at the top of the paper, "Dallas-Ft Worth Int'l, E-32."

"Where on earth could he be sending me?" she wondered. She felt a certain dread, and an exhilaration, like a school girl anticipating her first date. With uncharacteristic obedience (obedience was one of the things she was working on) she packed her suitcase.

Rob was waiting for her at gate E-32. The marquee behind the check-in desk promised Honolulu. Rob draped a lei around her neck, a real flower lei. Where he found a lei in Texas, she never knew.

"What's the stocking cap for?" Annie asked as they buckled their seatbelts.

"It's cold on top of a volcano." Rob replied, a twinkle in his eye.

Task Three: Grieve the Particular Losses of This Passage

_____ "I understand and practice the process of grieving."

_____ "I have come to peace with my relationship with my parents, whether they're living or dead."

_____ "I can think of good and bad times that I have had with my parents."

_____ "We have an empty nest."

_____ "I enjoy our children, but I'm glad they are out of our house."

_____ "I try not to be overinvolved in our children's lives."

_____ "My spouse and I both enjoy the freedom with out the kids."

_____ "We aren't supporting our grown children."

_____ "If our marriage is childless, we have grieved and resolved this void."

_____ "We have a workable plan for retirement."

_____ "We can live on our budget in retirement."

_____ "We have appropriate boundaries with our adult children."

_____ "I have found some exciting opportunities as my life emphasis shifts from career and childrearing to new frontiers."

_____ "I accept the physical changes in my body and grieve the loss of my youth."

_____ "I have resolved my friendships with others and have 'mended what needed mending.' "

_____ "I understand how vital grieving is to a healthy life."

How well have you dealt with the losses in your life during this Fourth Passage? If you could check most of the above statements we'd say very well. However, if you, like most of us, have a hard time accepting and resolving the losses associated with middle age, you probably couldn't check all the above statements.

Grief is an ongoing process. It's not over and done with, quick and dirty. You will likely find yourself recycling back through the steps of grief several times. And, that's healthy, you are letting yourself feel and purge the pain from the loss. Years afterwards, a friend of ours related that she felt incredible sadness over her father's death. She thought she had mourned the death, and she may have, but something triggered that grief and she was back in the sadness step again.

Another example: grief over the loss of a job by a client of ours was stalemated in the depression stage. For two years this man was stalled in this second step. Fortunately, he sought out help and we could begin to help him progress further in his grieving.

Likewise, if you still feel the effects of a loss and it's been several months, maybe even several years, we suggest you seek outside guidance—a pastor, a trusted friend, or a professional therapist. You need the freedom to resolve these losses before you can embrace the gains of this passage. Use whatever tools you can to resolve them.

Things to Avoid at This Stage of Your Relationship

Dr. Debi Newman has compiled the following bits of information to help you through the Fourth Passage. The following are areas that you and your spouse should avoid like the plague. They can be real marriage-killers.

1. Getting Overinvolved in Your Adult Children's Lives—
   Financially and/or Emotionally
   A woman we'll call Marla played a tightrope game between her new husband and her widowed mother. Her mother felt free to pop in on her daughter and son-in-law anytime. "Oh, don't bother," she would say as she barged right in, "It's only me."

Wearied beyond patience by this constant invasion of their privacy, Marla's husband found a job in Minneapolis, a thousand miles away. Six months later Mom retired, to Minnesota.

And so the unhealthy codependent relationship between Mom and daughter and now son-in-law continued and escalated. For your children's sakes, for your own sake, and for your marriage's sake, draw and uphold appropriate boundaries between their lives and yours. Do the following as an exercise to draw those boundaries:

Boundaries with Adult Children

We agree on the following boundaries with our adult children:

a. Babysitting for our grandchildren (how much, when, where):

_____

_____

b. Giving gifts of money (how much, for what purposes, how often):

_____

_____

c. Supporting our adult children financially (what are the sideboards, loan terms, ceiling amount): _____

_____

_____

d. Calling and visiting (how often, uninvited or invited): __

_____

_____

Susan Hemfelt explains, "You've got to be able to say 'no' to both your children and your grandchildren. Don't feel guilty about it. You've served your time, per se; you raised them, now enjoy your freedom. Make your time your own. That way you'll savor the time you have with your children or your grandchildren because it won't feel like an imposition.

"And, don't suppress your resentment towards your children's requests. That will only make matters worse. Calmly and carefully explain to them the need for boundaries and then decide on those boundaries if you haven't already."

2. Not Setting Up a Support System of Friends, but Being Only Centered Around Your Spouse

We briefly touched on this in the last chapter when we discussed how Annie focused on Rob for her entertainment and socializing once Beth Anne was gone. That can be deadly. True intimacy allows the person you love to have the freedom to pursue his or her own dreams and interests without having you along all the time. You need to loosen your grip on each other before it becomes a vise grip and is wrenched apart by one or the other of you.

Too, as you develop your own set of friends and interests apart from your spouse, you are preparing for eventual separation from your spouse. As painful as that will be, it will happen sooner or later.

As you develop your circle of friends, be sure to have friends of all ages. Don't isolate yourself to just one age group. As valuable as they are as a support group, your mind will be more challenged and expanded by friendships with persons both much younger and much older than you and your husband.

Take the opportunity afforded you by increased free time and develop some individual interests and talents. It's never too late to start something you've always wanted to do.

Annie Warden Millen took some creative writing classes. She always loved writing. In fact, she frequently edited newsletters for her volunteer organizations. During Annie's school years, teachers encouraged her to do something with her writing. Instead, she followed the needs of her family. But now she could write, and what a treasure chest of experience she could bring to that writing.

3. Not Planning for Retirement

Reread Chapter Eight if you don't understand what we mean here. Don't be caught off guard when retirement hits, financially or emotionally. It's imperative that *both* of you take an active role in this planning.

Susan Hemfelt's father recommends that all couples in

their Fourth Passage make a concentrated effort to get completely out of debt and stay out of debt. He also recommends that you study your life insurance situation, update your wills, and make final funeral arrangements for each other. It also might be a time to look into nursing home insurance if you can afford it.

4. Blaming Each Other and Living in the Past Rather than Building a Growing, Happy Relationship

As Susan Hemfelt says, "Identify and dispense with any lingering disappointments, resentments, and unrealistic expectations you have about yourself, your spouse, and your marriage. Write them down, every little hurt. If necessary, read them aloud to God when you pray. Then let them go, grieve them through. Ask God's help. Forgive yourself, your spouse and your marriage for all its shortcomings."

Laying aside the blame and forgiving opens up the way for intimacy between the two of you. Remember the equation:

Forgiveness = resolved anger.
As opposed to:
Unresolved anger = resentment.
and
Resentment turned inward = depression.

Guard, then, against depression by resolving the anger in your life through forgiveness.

There's Nowhere to Go but Forward

New Love, the first two years. Realistic Love, the third through the tenth year. Steadfast Love, the eleventh through the twenty-fifth year. Renewing Love, the twenty-six through the thirty-fifth year. You've been together a long time now, longer than with any other person.

How well do you know each other? Take the following fun quiz to see. Debi and Brian Newman use these types of quizzes frequently in their work with other couples.

Answer each question for you and for your spouse. Have

your partner do the same. Then compare your answers to
see how well you know each other.

1. What would you say is your worst habit? _____
2. What would your spouse say is your worst habit? _____
3. What memories do you treasure most about your marriage? _____
4. What memories does your spouse treasure most about
   your marriage? _____
5. What accomplishment are you most proud of? _____
6. What accomplishment is your spouse most proud of? _
7. What was a favorite car that you owned? _____
8. What was a favorite car of your spouse's? _____
9. Which one of your relatives do you like the most? ____
10. Which one of your relatives does your spouse like the
    most? _____
11. What is your most treasured memory of your wedding
    day? _____
12. What is your spouse's most treasured memory of your
    wedding day? _____
13. How do you like your steak (or egg if you don't eat
    steak) cooked? _____
14. How does your spouse like his/her steak (or egg)
    cooked? _____
15. What is the nicest gift you ever received? _____
16. What is the nicest gift your spouse ever received? _____

Looking Ahead

The final passage lies ahead: Transcendent Love. True
love at last. Dr. Hemfelt explains that you don't really know
what transcendent love is until you're there. "It's like trying
to describe ice cream. You can lecture for hours and hours
about the physical components of ice cream, how to make it
and what it looks like. But you can't tell anyone what it
tastes like, until they've actually tasted it and experienced it
firsthand.

"Similarly, I can hear about the peace of this transcendent

love in my youth, but I cannot possibly know what it is until I have the maturity, the wisdom, the life experience to get the concept of transcendent love from my head into my heart."

That's what to look forward to: A love more deep and profound than the day you were married. You will truly reach a higher plane of intimacy with this other person.

Not dependency but oneness.

About the Authors

Dr. Frank Minirth is a diplomate of the American Board of Psychiatry and Neurology. Along with Dr. Paul Meier, he founded the Minirth-Meier Clinic in Dallas, Texas, one of the largest psychiatric clinics in the United States.

Mary Alice Minirth is a homemaker and the mother of four children.

Dr. Brian Newman is the clinical director of inpatient services at the Minirth-Meier Clinic in Richardson, Texas. He received his M.A. in counseling from Grace Theological Seminary and his Doctorate of Philosophy from Oxford Graduate School.

Dr. Deborah Newman is a psychotherapist with the Minirth-Meier Clinic. She received her M.A. in counseling from Grace Theological Seminary and her Doctorate of Philosophy from Oxford Graduate School.

Dr. Robert Hemfelt is a psychologist with the Minirth-Meier Clinic who specializes in the treatment of chemical dependencies and compulsivity disorders.

Susan Hemfelt is a homemaker and the mother of three children.